ACTIVATORS

Classroom Strategies for

Engaging Students

Middle and High School

Activators: Classroom Strategies for Engaging Middle and High School Students
By Nicole Frazier and Donna Mehle
© 2013 Educators for Social Responsibility

esr

Educators for Social Responsibility
23 Garden Street
Cambridge MA 02138
www.esrnational.org

Book design by Walter Zekanoski / WZ DESIGN

10 9 8 7 6 5 4 3 2 1
Printed in the United States of America

ISBN 13: 978-0-942349-71-9

ACTIVATORS

Classroom Strategies for Engaging Middle and High School Students

Nicole Frazier and **Donna Mehle**

Foreword by **Carol Ann Tomlinson**

esr

EDUCATORS *for* SOCIAL RESPONSIBILITY

Contents

Foreword

Each year at the University of Virginia, I teach a class that focuses students on thinking about the nature of effective curriculum. I sometimes begin the class by asking students to think about a class they've experienced in which the curriculum—the contents or ideas they explored—were memorable to them, and then to write a brief vignette or explanation that would help a colleague understand why the curriculum in that class was meaningful for them. In giving the directions, I take care to focus students on the curriculum that was at the heart of the class.

It's the first day in the class, and students work with evident concentration on the writing assignment. When I ask them to form groups of about four to share their writing, it's clear that they enjoy both sharing their experiences and hearing the experiences of their peers. I give the groups several questions to discuss after the sharing and learn a great deal about the entry points of the various students into a class on curriculum design as I walk among the groups and listen in on their dialogue.

The real intrigue of the activity for me happens, however, when the class as a whole shares the attributes of compelling curriculum based on their individual writing and small group exchanges. Never in the years that I've used the activity has the list the students generated contained descriptors of curriculum. Rather, virtually every student every time describes a dynamic teacher or engaging instruction. It is as though the students have no idea at all what course they've signed up to take.

In his book *Visible Learning: A Synthesis of 800 Meta-analyses Relating to Achievement*, John Hattie says, "…pedagogy trumps curriculum. Or more precisely, pedagogy is curriculum, because what matters is how things are taught, rather than what is taught." At another point, his research findings cause him to reiterate, "It is less the content of curricula that is important than the strategies teachers use to implement the curriculum so that students progress upwards through the curricula content."

Now, I'm a certified curriculum geek. I love the reality that a teacher is a weaver of meaning, expert in the process of taking information that may, at first glance, seem remote to young people (or adults) and crafting it into sequences and narratives and ideas that can ultimately help learners find meaning in the world around them and in their own existence. I want to believe I can help educators re-conceptualize the power of a teacher by coming to understand that excellent teachers only serve up curriculum that invites young minds to a feast of understanding. In other words, I should be concerned, if not offended, that my new crop of students in a curriculum design course completely ignores curriculum and focuses instead on instruction.

In truth, I've taught long enough to conclude that John Hattie is correct. What's memorable to us about a class is a combination of the teacher's connections with his or her students and that teacher's capacity to involve or engage students. In other words, instruction breathes life into curriculum, and it's those moments when instruction plugs our minds into universal ideas, issues, or insights that live on, well past the end of a grade level or school year.

So along with curriculum, I'm also a celebrant of vibrant instruction. That sort of instruction does not result from a teacher collecting assorted instructional strategies from conferences or books of classroom gimmicks. Rather, it stems from careful selection of strategies by teachers who match them to the needs of students, the nature of the content those students must learn, and the context of the classroom. It's that synergy, in combination with the electricity of a teacher who is continually amazed both by the richness of what he or she teaches and the unfolding capacity of the people he or she teaches, that can produce great results.

This book is a "keeper" because it commends instructional strategies that engage the minds of adolescent learners as it attends to their need for interaction with and appreciation of peers. Further, the book reminds us at every turn that what we're teaching (curriculum) has to be a match for how we teach (instruction). In addition, it reflects an understanding of the persistent classroom reality that there is no strategy that can free teachers from the need to plan thoughtfully for implementation of that strategy.

Activators: Classroom Strategies for Engaging Middle and High School Students reminds us that the classroom is a system with interdependent parts and that we succeed in our mission as teachers only when we take care with each of the parts. It instructs readers with rigorous attention to the interconnectedness of quality curriculum, thoughtful instruction, detailed attention to classroom management, and student success.

I would have been a grateful student of *Activators* during the two decades that I taught in middle school and high school. I look forward to introducing it to my university students.

Carol Ann Tomlinson
William Clay Parrish, Jr. Professor and Chair of Educational Leadership,
Foundations, and Policy
Curry School of Education, University of Virginia

Preface

There is growing evidence and recognition that high standards and rigorous expectations must be couched in the context of engaging classrooms in order for every student to thrive, achieve, and excel. According to a 2004 report on Engaging Schools from the National Research Council and the Institute of Medicine, students who are not engaged in school are at higher risk for poor academic achievement, attendance problems, and dropping out.

Academic engagement is especially critical for adolescent learners. A 2013 Gallup Student Poll showed that student engagement drops steadily from elementary through high school. Research shows that student engagement improves academic achievement, increases resiliency, lowers dropout rates, and reduces risky behavior such as sexual activity and substance abuse. Students' attitudes toward learning, motivation to participate, and choice to exert effort are all influenced by factors that are especially important in adolescence like learning readiness, prior knowledge, personal interest, and a sense of belonging and connectedness with other students and the teacher.

Educators for Social Responsbility works with middle and high school educators in a wide variety of settings across the country to reach and engage all learners. When we use the term academic engagement we are referring to sustained learning that involves students emotionally, cognitively and behaviorally.

Engagement profoundly impacts learning and achievement in many ways. For example, it contributes to:

- Accurate processing of information
- Expanded working memory for problem solving and critical, creative, practical, and reflective thinking
- Increased capacity to store and retrieve information from long-term memory
- Increased interest, curiosity, and imagination
- Sustained effort to complete challenging work
- Greater self-direction and independence as a learner
- Increased value placed on academic goals, habits, tasks, and achievement
- Increased feelings of pride, competence, satisfaction, and enjoyment related to academic achievement

ESR has identified Six Conditions that Support Academic Engagement (see the Six Conditions on page ix). Our model takes into account emotional, cognitive, and behavioral dimensions of engagement that researchers have identified. Based upon this Six Conditions framework, we support teachers through professional learning and coaching to create conditions that foster academic engagement and increased levels of good will, attention, participation, interest, effort, and investment in learning.

Six Conditions of
Academic Engagement

Interest

Participation

Academic engagement is sustained learning that involves students emotionally, cognitively, and behaviorally.

Good Will

Effort

Investment

Attention

Engagement in learning results in greater academic achievement because it cultivates...

- Accurate processing of information
- Expanded working memory for problem solving and critical, creative, practical, and reflective thinking
- Increased capacity to store and retrieve data from long-term memory
- Sustained effort to complete challenging work
- Greater self-direction and independence as a learner
- Increased value placed on academic goals, habit, tasks, and achievement
- Increased feelings of pride, competence, satisfaction, and enjoyment related to academic achievement

ESR prides itself on offering practical strategies like Activators that bring "student engagement" to life in middle and high school classrooms. A teacher cannot achieve broad student engagement by flipping a switch. Instead, academic engagement is achieved over time through a wide range of learning strategies, instructional supports, and opportunities for social interaction, along with a positive climate and community of learners. Activators are a catalyst for fostering student engagement. They generally are short activities (two to twenty minutes) that can be used to introduce, make an important transition within, or wrap up a lesson. Activators have some significant qualities that align with what we know about student engagement and adolescent development. They prime the pump and help get students ready to learn. They tap into an adolescent's capacity and desire to think critically, reflect, and problem solve. They support the developmental need, interest, and desire of the adolescent learner to participate in active learning experiences and social interactions with peers.

ESR has a long history of supporting teachers with instructional strategies that bring students' voices into the room, incorporate movement, foster social interaction, and create community. Activators are often subject-area-specific and are used intentionally at different times to support a well-paced lesson. They help focus the group and help focus attention on the "big idea" or topic of the main lesson. Different methods for grouping make social interaction and time for reflection an even more purposeful part of the experience.

We are grateful to Nicole Frazier and Donna Mehle for making a powerful contribution to the continual enrichment of teaching and learning, and the advancement of practices that foster student engagement. They brought to the task their wisdom as former teachers, creativity, and a commitment to excellence, along with thoughtful, careful attention to and for their colleagues in the field. As a result, middle and high school teachers of all subjects have this unique, practical, and valuable new resource available to them to help engage their students.

Michele Tissiere
Director of Professional Services
Educators for Social Responsibility

Larry Dieringer
Executive Director
Educators for Social Responsibility

Authors' Note

We have been inspired by many sources as we developed content area examples for *Activators*. For a full list of credits listed by chapter and content area, please see the Credits section on page 237.

Certain words used in this book call for expanded definitions, which can be found in Appendix 1, Glossary of Key Terms, on page 205. Those words are marked when they first appear in this book with a flag icon⚑.

Acknowledgements

The writing of this book started with the initial intent of compiling tried and true strategies for ramping up student engagement. We soon had a number of effective strategies in mind—thanks to our colleagues past and present—and yet we knew that wouldn't be enough. We wanted to create a tool that was more than just a laundry list of learning strategies. Our goal was to create a book that would weave together the research on student engagement, high impact strategies for adolescent learners, the art of facilitation, and most importantly, practical examples so that teachers (and their students) could immediately start reaping the benefits of implementing Activators. A lofty goal perhaps, and one we wouldn't have attempted without the help and support of so many knowledgeable, committed, and inspiring educators.

We would like to thank Educators for Social Responsibility (ESR) for inviting us to undertake this writing project and for trusting and encouraging us to follow our vision as it unfolded. From the early design stages, we were given the freedom to take this book in a direction that we thought would be most helpful to teachers and students. We are so very thankful for ESR's foresight in having us co-author this book, laying the foundation for a special partnership that resulted in a dynamic where we could push each others' thinking and support each other with our different strengths. This team effort resulted in a book than neither of us could have written on our own, and we are each better writers and thinkers as a result of this collaborative experience.

We would like to thank Larry Dieringer, ESR's Executive Director, whose collaborative spirit and smart decisions in leading the organization has made this project possible.

This book rests steadily on the broad shoulders of ESR Senior Professional Services Consultant Carol Miller Lieber, whose in-depth analysis and synthesis of academic engagement research was foundational to our writing. Carol's keen understanding of both adolescents and effective instructional practices has informed our thinking every step of the way. It is not an overstatement to say that this book would not have been possible without her.

We appreciate the ongoing support of Michele Tissiere, ESR's Director of Professional Services. Michele's deep respect for teachers and careful attention to language has shaped who we are as program consultants and writers. She was a driving force behind the creation of this book and kept us anchored to the vision of creating a valuable tool for classroom teachers. When we encountered a challenge, we picked up the phone to call Michele, who never hesitated to answer. Her wisdom informs much of what you'll find in the book, and we are deeply grateful to her.

We would like to thank Jane Ellison for suggesting the name for the title of the book and learning strategies we now call "Activators." Over the years we have referred to some of these strategies as "Gatherings," some as "Move 'em or Lose 'em Strategies," and still others as "Engagement Strategies" or "Total Participation Strategies." None of these names seemed to completely convey the intent and results of each strategy. Jane helped us find a name that succinctly captured the essence of this practice.

We would also like to thank ESR professional consultants whose contributions have shaped this book. Nina Dibner and Lisa Cureton's early advice helped us explore ways of developing a book that would best serve classroom teachers. Kerry Lord brought to bear her classroom experience in reviewing science example Activators; and Naomi Migliacci helped us consider important ways these learning strategies support English Language Learners.

ESR staff members and interns have provided invaluable support in making this book become a reality. In particular we would like to thank Director of Marketing and Sales, Denise Wolk, for providing feedback on the manuscript at a key point in the writing process and interns Charlie Feick, Lela Rosen, and Anoush Arakelian for the spot-on research they conducted. Most importantly, we are grateful for Director of Publications, Jill Davidson, whose understanding, patience, and flexibility got us through each hurdle we faced safe and sound.

We would like to give a great big thank you to Kari Kokka, for her expertise with many of the Algebra and Geometry examples found in the book. We also appreciate math educator Geoffrey Enriquez for aligning the Activator examples with the Common Core State Standards. Math teachers Paul Asjes, Winston Gayle, Galo Reyes, and Wendy Santana each stepped in at just the right moment to contribute an example, resource or idea for refining the wording of a math problem. And the science examples wouldn't have been possible without the generous help and smart thinking of science teacher Kaitlin Finn. We are grateful to all of them for sharing their content area expertise.

We are deeply grateful to Michele Morris Jones, Wendy Ward Hoffer, and Laura Thomas for offering their educational expertise in reading the manuscript at a critical juncture. The insightful, constructive feedback we received from each of them helped us sharpen our thinking and reminded us of what our audience needed from us as writers.

A special thank you goes to our family and friends for their support and understanding during the writing process. They provided much needed encouragement along the way and allowed some other things to take a backseat when we had deadlines to meet and conference calls that lasted hours longer than anticipated.

In closing, we'd like to offer our sincere appreciation for all educators who have labored to create engaging classrooms and whose work has informed the Activators you'll find in this book. Teaching is inherently collaborative; we have borrowed from and have been inspired by those who came before us and who probably adapted from others. We certainly take no credit for inventing these Activators and thank all teachers, past and present, known and unknown, who have helped shaped these strategies.

Nicole Frazier and **Donna Mehle**

> *When students are engaged and motivated and feel minimal*
> *stress, information flows freely through the affective filter in the*
> *amygdala and they achieve higher levels of cognition, make connections,*
> *and experience "aha" moments. Such learning comes not from quiet*
> *classrooms and directed lectures, but from classrooms*
> *with an atmosphere of exuberant discovery.*
>
> –ALFIE KOHN

ACTIVATORS:
AN INTRODUCTION

What Are Activators?

Activators are learning strategies that incorporate think time and purposeful social interaction to foster emotional, cognitive, and behavioral engagement. Let's step into a ninth grade biology classroom to see how a well-facilitated Activator can deepen students' learning and support academic achievement.

The passing bell rings. Mr. Martinez stands at the door greeting his students as they enter, "Congratulations on yesterday's game, Crystal. Good to see you, James." Students chat as they make their way to their seats, but once the bell rings they fall into the established routine, silently read the posted directions and begin a task designed to deepen their understanding around yesterday's lesson on cell organelles and their functions. Students are seated in groups of four and on their desks are sets of cards. Written directions explain that they have two minutes to independently write down two things they remember from yesterday's lesson on using a city analogy to understand cell organelle functions. Mr. Martinez sets a timer and positions himself in a space that allows him to scan the room to see which students might need help getting on task. He then circulates and redirects students who haven't gotten started yet, "It sounds like you're concerned about how you did on your history quiz last period, Candace. I'm confident you want to do well on this week's biology quiz; check out the directions on the board and please get started." As the two minutes come to a close, the timer goes off, and Mr. Martinez signals it is time to finish up by slowly counting down, "5,4,3,2,1." Students focus their attention on Mr. Martinez who continues, "Please look at the directions on the board—your task is to work as a group and use the cards on your desks to match up the organelle name with its function, image, and city structure analogy we learned about yesterday. You now have three minutes to complete the task. Please begin." Having engaged in card sorts several times since the beginning of the year, students start spreading the cards out on their desks so everyone can see them and soon start talking with their group members about how to match them up. Mr. Martinez moves around the room, jotting down notes as he listens to students' conversations: "Why is the nucleus like city hall?" "I think this might be the vacuole—it has a big space where it can store stuff." "What do the mitochondria do again?"

As the three minutes come to a close, Mr. Martinez invites everyone to finish up their conversations by again counting down, "Five, four, three, two, one." Once he has the group's attention, he calls on two groups of students who sorted their cards differently to share their reasons with the class. Afterwards, he asks a few students to assess the groups' responses, "What do you think about the two different ways the groups sorted the cards? Which one would you say is correct and what evidence might you offer to support your answer?" After the correct answer has been determined, Mr. Martinez then addresses the group that sorted the cards incorrectly, "Mistakes are great opportunities for all of us to clarify our thinking in preparation for this week's quiz. Tell us what you learned from listening to your peers." Once Mr. Martinez is confident that his students understand the different cell organelle functions, he affirms their effort by saying, "I love how you were really wrestling with the difference between the cell membrane and the cell wall. Now let's move on to today's lesson."

Mr. Martinez taps into adolescent learners' desire to problem-solve and socially interact by using a Card Sort Activator to deepen their understanding of the functions of cell organelles. By asking them to collaborate on this multisensory task, they experience emotional, cognitive, and behavioral engagement in learning. Mr. Martinez's effective facilitation was as important as his choice of strategy for strengthening his students' engagement. After initially garnering their good will by meeting and greeting them at the door, Mr. Martinez gets and keeps his ninth graders' attention through providing clear directions, using a timer, and circulating to listen in on their thinking. Collecting data during the Activator allows him to facilitate a debriefing, which deepens all students' understanding and feelings of efficacy.

A Card Sort is just one example of the variety of Activator formats available to teachers looking to ramp up student engagement. Activators might take the form of a simple and strategically placed Turn and Talk (Chapter 4) or incorporate manipulatives like Mini

Whiteboard (Chapter 8) or the Card Sort (Chapter 9). Others require students to get out of their seats and move, like Toss One, Take One (Chapter 10) and Opinion Continuum (Chapter 12). Depending upon the format and extent of the debriefing, Activators can last between two and twenty minutes. And while Mr. Martinez started his lesson with an Activator, it can just as well occur at the middle or end, based upon the teacher's purpose.

Although Activators have different formats, they all share two key components—individual think time and purposeful social interaction. Research has repeatedly shown that intentional "wait time" or "think time" results in significant benefits to student learning including increased number of student responses, length and accuracy of responses, and use of evidence to support responses (Rowe, 1972; Stahl, 1990; Tobin, 1987). In addition, the purposeful social interaction at the heart of each Activator provides structured cooperative learning opportunities which studies have shown results in average gains of seventeen percent in student achievement of targeted outcomes (Dean, Hubbell, Pitler, & Stone, 2012). So the essential ingredients of each Activator are research-based best practices that are proven methods for impacting student achievement.

Let's further explore the variety of reasons a middle or high school teacher might integrate one or more Activators into a lesson.

Why Use Activators?

1. Activators Increase Engagement in Learning

Student engagement is more than involvement or participation. It means sustained learning involving academic and social behaviors that support a positive emotional state, heightened concentration, and exerted effort, all of which result in deep cognitive processing. Activators impact the six conditions required for engagement in learning by creating a state of "relaxed alertness." This state is necessary for deep cognitive processing and sustained behavioral involvement in a task (Caine, Caine, McClintic, & Klimek, 2005). While some Activators support certain conditions more than others and individual students benefit from Activators in different ways, the strategic and consistent use of Activators in support of daily learning outcomes[*] and the creation of a High-Performing Community of Learners[*] leads to increased engagement and academic achievement for all students.

Please refer to the Six Conditions for Academic Engagement graphic on page ix.

2. Activators Support a Well-Paced Lesson

A well-paced lesson that sustains the engagement of students includes a variety of grouping structures, learning strategies[*] and instructional supports[*], broken into a series of time chunks. An Activator quickly injects energy into the classroom by grouping students in different ways and providing opportunities for students to interact with each other. Activators can front-load conditions needed for engagement at the beginning of a lesson, sustain these conditions at midpoints along the way, or reinforce them at the end of a lesson. And because Activators come in a variety of formats, they can be incorporated into any type of lesson to support pacing, including the workshop model, lectures, reviews, cooperative learning, or during projects.

3. Activators Create a High-Performing Community of Learners

Creating a High-Performing Community of Learners that results in a positive and personalized learning environment includes three key elements: building Trust and Belonging, establishing and maintaining Classroom Expectations[■] and Classroom Agreements[■], and supporting Habits of Learning. Activators are critical supports for all three elements.

Building Trust and Belonging

At the beginning of the year, Activators help students learn names, discover commonalities, and respect differences. This builds trust and belonging, which create a positive environment necessary for learning to take place (Sousa & Tomlinson, 2010; Willis, 2007). Throughout the year, Activators continue to foster these conditions that sustain a high-performing community, as students continue to share who they are as learners, value their peers as resources, and repeatedly understand that their voices and thinking are welcomed and valued.

Establishing and Maintaining Classroom Expectations and Classroom Agreements

At the beginning of a course, setting and communicating Classroom Expectations, which are beliefs that a teacher holds about what students are capable of doing and achieving, promotes positive social norms and a culture of excellence that is at the heart of teaching and learning. An example of a Classroom Expectation might be, "*I expect you to put forth your best effort.*" Activators can be used for students to make meaning of Classroom Expectations at the start of the year as well as to continually reflect on how they are living up to these over time.

For detailed examples of Classroom Expectations and Classroom Agreements and instructions on how to co-construct them with your students, refer to http://www.esrnational.org/activators.

It is also critical to encourage student ownership over desired classroom behaviors by using Activators to design Classroom Agreements, which are a negotiated set of behaviors and actions between the students and teacher about the ways in which the class will work together. For example, students and the teacher might create a Classroom Agreement that says, "*Let people finish what they have to say before someone else speaks.*" When teachers work in grade level teams, Classroom Agreements can be created across a grade in order to provide a more consistent experience for students. In order for Classroom Agreements to be touchstones that continue to guide a High-Performing Community of Learners, they must be revisited frequently. Activators offer ways of regularly reflecting on and monitoring Classroom Agreements throughout the year.

Supporting Habits of Learning

A High-Performing Community of Learners supports students in developing Habits of Learning[■] that lead to success in middle and high school and support postsecondary readiness. These can include Habits of Participation, Habits of Work, Habits of Discipline, Habits of Communication, and Habits of Mind (for examples of specific Habits of Learning, see Appendix 3.)

Activators reinforce these habits and result in improved social-emotional learning skills, including increased self-awareness, self-monitoring, social awareness, relationship skills, and responsible decision-making, which are the Collaborative for Social, Emotional Learning (CASEL) Core Competencies. Regular use of Activators around Habits of Learning provides opportunities for students to reflect on their progress and increases student accountability for practicing and developing proficiency with these habits.

4. Activators Generate Connections to Prior Knowledge

The brain processes information by making connections to what it already knows (Tokuhama-Espinosa, 2008). Helping students build bridges between new content and prior knowledge is critical for increasing a learner's motivation to process information and monitor comprehension. Activators are a handy tool for breaking open new content because they offer a variety of ways for students to reflect on and share with classmates what they already know at the beginning of a lesson or unit.

5. Activators Provide Opportunities to Practice Skills and Deepen Understandings

Students require multiple and varied opportunities to practice skills and engage with content through social interaction in order to construct meaning (Vygotsky, 1978) and store information in long-term memory. Integrating Activators into lessons throughout a unit allows students to interact with content and their classmates in a variety of compelling ways that increase their capacity to easily recall information and make new skills automatic.

6. Activators Support Formative Assessment

By putting student voice front and center, Activators provide an opportunity for real-time feedback for learning, often described as formative assessment[■]. As teachers listen to and observe students, they can gather data that help affirm understandings, uncover misconceptions and offer corrective feedback. Research emphasizes that providing this type of timely, focused feedback has significant impact on student learning and achievement, improving assessment results by an average of 28 percent (Dean et al., 2012; Marzano, 2009). When engaged in an Activator, students are also reflecting on debrief questions and listening to their peers in ways that encourage them to self-assess and make adjustments in their thinking. Students who receive this opportunity for metacognitive feedback have been shown to outperform students who only receive results (a simple grade or correct/incorrect feedback) (Dean et al., 2012). In addition, this type of low-stakes, ungraded formative assessment can reduce stress and help students gain confidence that increases the likelihood of increased performance on higher-stakes assessments (Sousa & Tomlinson, 2010).

7. Activators Prepare Students for Assessments

Activators help students review prior to an assessment, whether it is a test, presentation, or project—sending a strong signal that effort matters. The social nature of an Activator goes a long way in dispelling students' notions that just looking over notes is sufficient for their brains to store and retrieve information required on a final assessment. As a result, Activators provide an important opportunity for teachers to model, teach, practice, and assess students' use of active learning strategies.

8. Activators Inject Relevance into Curriculum

"Why do I have to learn this?" Adolescents love to ask this question. And whenever teachers can provide a satisfying response, engagement and achievement increase. That's because a learner's positive emotional reaction to information they consider relevant increases the probability that the information will sink in (Immordino-Yang & Faeth, 2010). Activators can inject a strong dose of relevance into the classroom by forging connections between course content and students' lives, futures, other disciplines, or the larger society.

Activators Support All Students

Incorporating Activators into your lessons will increase academic engagement and achievement for all students, including English Language Learners and Students with Special Needs. While both groups encompass a wide variety of learner profiles, the components of each Activator and the facilitation steps we provide support both groups with their unique learning needs.

Activators serve English Language Learners in three key ways. They provide varied opportunities for students to practice using English for authentic communication in meaningful and motivating contexts. The ongoing formative assessment that linguistically diverse learners receive while engaging in Activators is also critical for developing full proficiency with academic English. In addition, Activators offer opportunities for English Language Learners to comprehend texts through discussions and peer interaction. (Goldenberg, 2008).

By incorporating many effective special education interventions, Activators provide proven supports for students with disabilities (Scruggs, Mastropieri, Berkeley, & Graetz, 2010). Activators offer this student population practice in self-regulation, which is critical for increasing performance by encouraging students to monitor and assess comprehension, detect misunderstandings and correct mistakes (Zimmerman, 2001). Additional cognitive strategies embedded in Activators that support students with diverse learning needs include 1) rehearsing key information verbally, visually or kinesthetically, 2) using aids to organize, sequence and categorize information (Card Sorts) and 3) transforming information into visual or kinesthetic images (Image Cards, Post It Up, Opinion Continuum, Are You More Like), (Jordan, 2013). The latter two prove to be helpful strategies for English Language Learners as well (Hill & Flynn, 2006).

Flexibility and adaptability are key to effective instruction and the variations and extensions offered for each Activator format provide ways for teachers to make modifications and deepen learning to meet the diverse needs of all students in their classrooms.

Activators offer English Language Learners:
- practice using language for authentic communication
- peer interactions to promote reading comprehension
- frequent formative assessment
- opportunities to develop proficiency with academic English

Activators provide Students with Special Needs:
- practice in self-regulation
- ways of transforming information into visual or kinesthetic images
- aids to organize, sequence and categorize information
- rehearsal of key information verbally, visually or kinesthetically

How to Use This Book

Teachers always seek out new and varied practices to get their students excited about their discipline. As a result, you might be tempted to scan the Table of Contents and flip to one of the Activator chapters that pique your interest. We encourage you to "go slow to go fast" and read Chapters 2, 3 and 4 before moving on in order to experience the full benefits of this core practice in your classroom.

In Chapter 2, Questions to Consider Before Getting Started, we pose some key questions to help you reflect on the ways your current instructional approach and classroom conditions are a good fit for Activators as well as any modifications that you might want to consider before integrating them into your practice. Chapter 3, Facilitating Activators for Maximum Impact, provides some tips for supporting effective student participation in Activators; Chapter 4, Foundational Activators, includes three formats that build students' capacity to participate in Activators found later in this book; and Chapter 5, Activators to Kick-Start Your Year, offers some tried and true Activators that establish a High-Performing Community of Learners at the beginning of a course.

Chapters 6–17 each describe a different Activator and are sequenced according to the increasing level of complexity for the teacher in terms of necessary preparation and amount of student movement.

Within each of the Activators chapters (6–17) we include:

- A brief description and overview of the Activator
- Conditions for engagement that the Activator fosters
- A teacher prep list
- An Activator snapshot sketch to show how you will need to arrange students or your classroom
- Sample student directions to display
- Detailed teacher directions broken down into three parts: Set up the Activator, Model and Teach, and Practice and Assess
- Troubleshooting tips
- Variations and extensions
- Reasons for implementing the Activator along with content area examples
- A chart of content area examples for math, science, social studies, English language arts, and world languages
- Suggestions for writing your own content area Activators
- Work space for designing your own content area Activators

You will notice that we offer very specific directions for each Activator, since effective facilitation is critical for maximum student engagement. Some readers may choose to read these word-for-word and rehearse prior to introducing an Activator format to their students, while others may scan the directions to get the gist before incorporating one into tomorrow's lesson. While we provide core content examples for most Activators, if an Activator is not a good fit for a particular discipline, it is not included in the chapter.

We have also included several Appendices to support your ability to use this book with maximum effectiveness. Appendix 1 contains a Glossary of Key Terms used throughout the book. In Appendix 2 you will find alignment of the book's core content Activator examples to the Common Core Math and English Language Arts State Standards. Appendices 3 and 4 offer overviews of Habits of Learning and Grouping Strategies. We have also included an Index listing all of the content area examples by topic or theme, the Activator to which they are aligned, and the page numbers where they can be found.

As we mentioned in the Acknowledgments section, we do not take credit for inventing any of these Activators. What we do offer here are Activators that we stand behind in terms of their capacity to ramp up engagement and student achievement. In our 25-plus combined years of teaching experience as well as our work as educational consultants who support middle and high school teachers around the country, we've witnessed up close the ways in which these Activator formats ignite students' attention and interest, maximize participation, and drive well-paced lessons that deepen learning in meaningful ways. Just as important, we offer detailed facilitation tips for each Activator that are critical for fostering the conditions necessary for engaging middle and high school students in active learning.

Our hope is that this text will become a well-worn workbook for you, a book where you log your own original prompts alongside our models. You might even be inspired to create your own Activator format in order to meet your students' and your course content's unique and ever-evolving needs.

We encourage you now to consider your current practice and classroom conditions prior to implementing Activators by turning to Chapter 2.

1

> *Building a culture of thinking and a strong learning community...takes hard work, dedication, continual reflection, and most of all a willingness to take risks and reach outside the comfort zone of established practices.*
> — Ron Ritchhart, Mark Church, and Karin Morrison

Questions to Consider Before Getting Started

The following questions are important to consider for integrating Activators into your classroom practice on a regular basis.

How can you maximize the impact of using Activators? We cannot stress enough the importance of using Activators to target your daily and unit learning outcomes. Activators are designed to create student engagement in support of learning and student achievement. To ensure that your efforts result in meaningful learning, it will be critical to craft thoughtful prompts and carefully design your Activators so that they push students to think deeply about your content and/or practice the skills essential to your unit of study.

How conducive is your room setup to student movement and having students work in small groups? If the answer is "very," you will be good to go with a wide range of Activators. If you need to tweak your room setup to create a classroom that supports social interaction and allows movement, you might consider experimenting with a setup that includes table groups or paired desks and allows you to open up some space around the periphery of your room. Unfortunately, we know that some classroom spaces are far from ideal, so we have attempted to detail modifications in the troubleshooting section of each Activator to help with challenging physical spaces. We also recommend investing some time in the beginning of your course to teach students how to help you set up the room into two or three arrangements that will support the various Activators you plan on using. This might mean displaying a classroom setup map so students can quickly help you reconfigure the room. These maps can be posted as reminders each time you facilitate the Activators. Alternatively, you might post icons to designate specific areas of the room for certain types of conversations. For example, if you plan on using Opinion Continuum (Chapter 12) and Are You More Like (Chapter 14), you might create a map that demonstrates a way to create a long, narrow, open space in your room to accommodate students standing in a line. If you plan on doing Post It Up (Chapter 6), Four (or more) Corners (Chapter 13), or Rotation Stations (Chapter 16) on a regular basis, you might use icons to designate four to six zones around the periphery of your room where groups of student can congregate easily.

How comfortable are you with students being out of their seats and talking? Throughout the book we will be making the case that both movement and purposeful social interactions are necessary ingredients for sustained and deep cognitive engagement. We also understand the real challenges of managing two or three dozen adolescents in complex spaces, ensuring they are on-task and learning. Depending upon your comfort level and classroom management skills, you might be good to go with any of the Activators—or you and your students might need to ease your way towards the Activators featured in the later chapters, which require a bit more movement than those in the earlier chapters. While some of our readers might be more comfortable with the Activators that don't require students to get out of their seats, we urge you to welcome a little "discomfort" for the sake of student learning. In our early years of teaching, we were not intentional about regularly incorporating movement into our lessons and we know now it was at the expense of student learning. Over the years our students, with their casual comments, end-of-the-year feedback forms, and performance on assessments, taught us what brain research has revealed—"that movement and cognition are powerfully connected" (Jensen, 1998). And when movement is used in combination with purposeful social interaction, the knowledge and skills are even more likely to stick (Vygotsky, 1978; Bandura, 1986).

How comfortable and skilled are your students with focused and productive small-group or partner dialogue? If the answer is limited, investing time upfront to model, teach, practice, and assess these skills is critical as they are integral to all of the Activators; Chapter 4 provides detailed instructions for doing this. The Turn and Talk can be a tool to gauge your group's readiness. If students struggle to look at each other and say much of anything even after writing something down prior to the interaction, you have a group that is going to need lots of practice and encouragement with being interactive. In this case you might have to say things like, *"Okay, I need each of you to share at least three full statements with each other. If you need to glance at your notes or ask a question, go* *right ahead, just be sure you keep the conversation going.*" If you have a group that is full of chatterboxes, you might need to rein them in and help them stay focused on academic dialogue. For example you might say, "*One great thing about this group is you love to share your ideas. I have noticed that sometimes we lose our focus and I need to make sure each of you is prepared and focused to stay on topic. I am asking that during the next two-minute Turn and Talk you will focus on responding to the prompt and staying on-topic. Thank you.*" No two classes will be the same and so you will need to differentiate your facilitation to support each group's needs.

What are some ways you can group students? We recommend making intentional decisions around grouping students to ensure the effectiveness of your lesson. Depending upon the Activator and the instructional goals, teachers might choose to 1) group students randomly, 2) provide some parameters for students to form their own groups, 3) intentionally or randomly group students using academic content or 4) intentionally group students based upon skills or strengths.

Using random strategies for grouping students creates opportunities for students to get to know and work with all of their classmates. Using these strategies also normalizes that students will work with a variety of partners while in your class and neutralizes you from the way students get matched up. Being able to work well with a variety of personalities is a life skill, so this also helps young people prepare for the expectations of college and careers. See suggestions for random grouping strategies such as counting off, using playing cards, puzzle pictures, or index cards in Appendix 4.

Sometimes you'll want to provide some parameters and allow students to form their own groups. This technique offers a degree of autonomy for students while encouraging them to form diverse groups and get to know their classmates, which supports their capacity to work together effectively. Suggestions for student self-grouping parameters are in Appendix 4 as well.

You might also intentionally or randomly create groups in ways that reinforce your course content. This can be done by creating one or more sets of grouping cards that students match up to form pairs, trios, or small groups. Examples for creating your own content area grouping cards can also be found at http://www.esrnational.org/activators.

There are times teachers may want to intentionally group students with similar skill levels or background knowledge in order to challenge them at a level that is best for them. At other times it might be more beneficial to create more diverse or balanced groups, so students experience working with peers who have different strengths and learning styles. The important thing is to vary the ways you intentionally group students to meet the different needs and interests of the young people in your classroom.

What are some ways to scaffold implementation? We strongly recommend starting with two or three creating community Activators over the course of a week to build trust and establish comfort within the group (see Chapter 5). Then, begin integrating some of the content area Activators, which can be found in Chapters 6–8. These require minimal preparation, are relatively easy for students to step into, or have fewer moving parts to facilitate. Finally, start to sprinkle in Activators that require slightly more preparation, movement, or challenge. Those can be found in Chapters 9-17. Keep in mind that while Card Sorts and Rotation Stations are examples of Activators that involve more initial preparation; they also yield high returns when it comes to student engagement and learning. Another plus is that the Card Sorts and materials for Rotation Stations can be used again from year to year.

Can I justify spending time on Activators given my curriculum load? Student engagement functions as a critical factor for deep learning, and Activators are a powerful tool to ensure learning readiness and engagement. If you teach without taking the time to do Activators or other types of engagement strategies, you run the risk of "covering content," resulting in student learning that is short-term and superficial. In direct contrast, Activators are a tool for pushing students to think deeply and engage in experiences that help them solidify their new knowledge and skills.

What is important to keep in mind when designing effective Activator prompts? When designing effective prompts, you will want to design prompts that 1) strategically align to your unit's learning outcomes, 2) foster conditions for engagement, and 3) use invitational language. To avoid the pitfall of Activators being just an activity you do in your classroom and ensure that this core practice drives deep learning, it is critical to align your Activator prompts to your course and unit learning outcomes. Unit plans help teachers make tough decisions about what to teach and how to teach it, keep them on pace to achieve unit goals, and support a cohesive learning experience. In order for Activators to become a key learning strategy that you consistently and strategically align with unit learning outcomes, consider tweaking your current unit plan template to include an Activators section. Depending upon when and where you place the Activators in your unit and daily lessons, they might be used to introduce unit content, serve as a step towards the desired learning outcomes, support higher-level thinking about the content, or help you assess if students have achieved the learning outcome.

You will also want to design prompts that foster conditions of engagement. In order to support **trust** and **belonging**, it is critical that all students can respond to an Activator prompt without feeling anxious or uncomfortable. To support **effort**, it is important to consider ways to craft prompts so that students have enough prior knowledge to feel competent in their responses. Sometimes your Activator prompts will simply help students develop initial understanding of the content and it is the movement or interaction of the Activator format that supports **attention** and **interest**. Using an Activator to support the understanding of key terms or main points would be an example of this. Whenever possible, though, we suggest fostering **attention** and **interest** with a prompt that ignites curiosity, makes content relevant and challenges students to think at a high level. For example, instead of asking *"What is globalization"* which might result in the regurgitation of a text book definition, a social studies teacher might ask students to respond to the question, *"What are some of the ways your future will be impacted by the trends of globalization?"* Designing compelling Activator prompts in this way will increase students' engagement and move them closer to the learning outcome.

Crafting prompts with invitational language encourages exploratory thinking by reducing the need for certainty (Cognitive Coaching Seminars). Open-ended questions, which cannot be answered with a simple "yes" or "no," are critical for communicating a positive expectation around students' productive responses during an Activator. For example, instead of asking, *"Is there a Classroom Agreement we're finding it easy to live up to?"* a teacher asks, *"What agreements are we having an easy time living up to?"* Another element of invitational language is the use of plural forms (*reasons* instead of *reason*, *examples* instead of *example*) in Activator prompts. This can free students up from immediately evaluating what the "best" answer is, in order to develop several options and support divergent thinking. Exploratory language (words like *might, some, hunches, seems*) also builds students' confidence in trying out ideas rather than having to defend thinking that they are still in the process of developing and rehearsing. When students go public with their responses to these prompts during the course of an Activator, the divergent thinking that they encounter encourages them to examine, refine, and deepen their own understandings.

Will Activators work with all student groups? If you have been in the classroom for more than a few years, you have probably experienced a class that just seemed to magically click—where everyone got along, participation was high, and you would have no qualms about integrating any of the Activators. Likewise, most teachers have experienced classes where the group dynamic is challenging and the idea of regular doses of movement and social interaction raises concerns. A key premise of this book is that group dynamics need not be something we credit to chance. By investing time to "build the group," you can cultivate the conditions that create a High-Performing Community of Learners with any mix of students. That last statement might cause a few of our readers to mumble, "They obviously haven't met my sixth period!" We certainly know and respect that some groups are more complicated than others and may provide unique challenges. We can also attest to the numerous times those "tough classes" turned out to be the ones that stick in our memories as some of the best; with intentional effort, an extremely challenging mix of students can become connected, curious, focused, and successful. Often, the groups with which we have the most concerns about implementing a new practice are actually those that are the most in need of that new approach. And by investing the time to model and teach the expectations for Activators with this type of class, they are able to step into this new practice with confidence and comfort.

How long will it take for me to start seeing results? You should expect initial results of using Activators to be highly contingent upon how comfortable your students are with participating and sharing their thinking. Trust is essential for students to be ready to learn, participate fully, and to engage in purposeful social interaction. It takes trust to harness the full potential of Activators, and Activators provide a piece of the infrastructure that will enable educators to build that level of trust with each student and within the group. While it might take a few weeks, consistent use of Activators will result in a classroom culture in which students enter expecting to participate, share their thinking, and engage fully in the lesson. And the more Activators become part of your classroom routine, the less energy students will expend on how to "do" them, which will help them focus more attention on the quality of their thinking and discourse with one another.

In Chapter 3, we will unpack what it is going to take to effectively facilitate Activators.

2

CHAPTER

The brain is a social brain. Mirror neurons…activate when you see someone doing something the same way as if you were doing it. This enables humans to learn by watching others, which is the way humans learned through most of human history.

— Dr. Janet Zadina

Facilitating Activators for Maximum Impact

This chapter will help teachers understand exactly what to expect and plan for in order to begin implementing and facilitating Activators strategically and effectively in any school, with any group of students.

Ideally, you will start the year using Activators consistently so you can establish immediately that "this is how we learn together." However, if it is mid-year and you are trying these strategies for the first time, we urge you to combine persistence with patience. Additionally, if this type and level of participation is a new experience for your students, they might initially feel self-conscious about speaking with their peers. Some might hold back, waiting to see if Activators will be a consistent practice and thus worth their effort. Building a foundation for trust requires an investment of time and effort that will ultimately draw significant returns.

First Things First

Before launching Activators in your classroom, take time to contemplate three conditions that will be foundational to successful implementation.

1. **Project confidence and conviction:** Classroom teachers know well that adolescents respond to hesitance with impressive stores of resistance. A teacher's belief in the practice of Activators is perhaps the most essential condition for success because it will impact their comfort level while facilitating and their persistence in helping students maximize the learning opportunities that Activators provide. Being confident and staying positive in the face of any resistance or teenage negativity is the antidote. Here's what that might sound like in the classroom:

   "Yesterday I explained the purpose of doing Turn and Talks and let you know we would frequently start class this way. I did hear a few folks grumbling about having to turn and talk to a partner and I can appreciate that this practice might be new or perhaps even a little uncomfortable for some of you. I want to remind you that from kindergarten to college and beyond, brain research has shown that talking about what you think and know helps you learn and understand at a deep level."

   This confident statement acknowledges resistance while simultaneously clarifying expectations and holding students accountable for meeting them.

2. **Establish procedures and routines for silent think time:** Because the first step in most Activators consists of independent processing time, it will be important to establish exactly how you expect students to respond to a prompt. Each student might have a composition book or a specific section in their binder where they journal or jot responses. The quality of think time impacts the success of an Activator because it provides that critical moment for each student to individually process their thoughts and be emotionally and cognitively "prepared" for the social interaction that supports deep learning. As teachers we need to build endurance in students' ability to focus and engage in independent think time. And since one-third to one-half of Americans are introverts (Caine, 2012) who thrive by processing their thinking independently, it is critical that teachers provide opportunities for this large percentage of their student population to develop their strengths.

3. **Establish and maintain Classroom Agreements:** While schools have rules they set and enforce and teachers establish their own Classroom Expectations, we recommend that teachers make time to co-construct Classroom Agreements with each class to guide learning and peer interactions. Classroom Agreements provide an opportunity for student voice which promotes ownership over the ways young people want to work and learn together. Clear Classroom Agreements will be the rudder that keeps your Activators on course.

Getting Started

Rarely do things go perfectly on the first go-around, so having a strategic plan to both introduce and implement a new strategy will be key to your success. We encourage you to consider the following facilitation and implementation suggestions before launching your use of Activators.

As with introducing any new procedure or routine, it is crucial to explicitly 1) **set up the Activator**, 2) **model and teach**, and 3) **practice and assess** it in order to achieve the desired outcomes. All of these steps support what it takes for the brain to tune in to the new information, process it accurately, and enable that new learning to stick in long-term memory. Let's explore each step in more detail within the context of a specific Activator example.

1. Set up the Activator

The first step is to be transparent around the purpose of the Activator. Adolescents crave relevance, and if they do not understand why they are doing something, they are unlikely to engage in it. Take a minute to let students know exactly why you are doing the activity and what you hope to achieve by it. This might sound like, "*We are doing the activity so that you can all deepen your understanding of two key algebraic concepts, to give you an opportunity to practice college and career readiness skills, and so we can learn from each other. I have high expectations that this type of activity will help us get smarter together.*"

Clarity of directions is a condition for success, and the first time you introduce a new Activator you will also need to provide clear and concise instructions. Taking the time to be overtly explicit with both written and verbal directions will ensure that students know exactly what they are expected to do for the specific Activator. Displaying student-friendly directions on the board, chart paper, or a slide, supports effective implementation. If students seem confused or off-task you can gesture towards the board and ask them to check the instructions or check in with another student.

Use a signal to get attention. The following examples work well with both middle and high school students.

1.) Teacher raises hand

2.) "5, 4, 3, 2, 1" countdown

3.) Chime or distinct sound

Ensuring that you have silence and everyone's attention before giving clear directions is a best practice that serves to support both classroom management and student engagement. We recommend using a consistent and developmentally appropriate signal that efficiently and respectfully communicates, "*Stop talking, stop what you're doing, and focus on me.*" Signals can be non-verbal (raised hand), verbal (5, 4, 3, 2, 1), or even incorporate a sound, like a chime. Because students deeply engaged in dialogue will often see you before they hear you, combining a verbal and nonverbal element to your signal can make it all the more effective. When teaching 11th and 12th graders, you might want to engage them in a conversation about what type of signal they consider age-appropriate that would get their attention. Whatever signal you use, it is important to be consistent, so that students' responses become automatic.

Let's take a look at what all of this might look and sound like in the classroom. Hold up fingers and slowly count down, "5, 4, 3, 2, 1." After a five-second silent pause, say, "*I need your attention and silence for two minutes while I give you*

instructions for an activity we will be doing two or three times a month in this class."
Gesture to the written directions you have on the board, and pause again to make sure you have students' attention before reviewing them. You might have to make a follow-up specific request, *"I'm waiting to have all eyes on the board and voices silent so I can review the instructions. Thank you."*

An added benefit to always giving directions two ways is that it serves as an antidote to the all too familiar and often exasperating *"What are we doing again?"* questions. Simply respond with eye contact and then point to the directions and say, *"Reread the directions and then if you need clarifications ask your partner first and then if you still need help I'll come check in with you."* Or you might reinforce the notion that their classmates are resources in a different way by calling on another student to restate the instructions for the whole class. If students know that instructions are always visible and that their peers are a good source of support, they are able to be more self-directed and will get in the habit of looking around to figure things out for themselves.

2. Model and Teach

Taking the time to be overtly explicit with **written and verbal** directions that also include a model or sample will ensure that students know exactly what they are expected to do for the specific Activator. It is important to acknowledge that sometimes you will begin by modeling, while at other times you might start by explicitly teaching expectations. This can be a fluid process that spirals, with the two steps often blending together.

We all learned to walk and talk without our parents writing out the steps on a whiteboard. The power of a live model is often the vital ingredient to ensuring complete understanding. And while all students benefit from modeling, this instructional support is critical for English Language Learners, anxious students and others with language processing issues. Modeling an Activator can include showing students how to move or physically position themselves, how to handle an object, showing a visual of what their notes might look like after listening to a partner or demonstrating how to communicate with a partner. Teachers might also model the cognitive moves involved in some Activators by doing a Think Aloud™ in which you talk through your thought process in detail, providing students with a model for the type of cognitive processing you are asking of them. Depending upon what aspect of the Activator you want to model, you can enlist a student volunteer or even a colleague who might be available and willing to help out. Some teachers might even think about showing video of previous classes in order to model effective engagement in an Activator.

If you are modeling a Turn and Talk Activator, in which a pair of students are sharing their thinking with each other, you might ask a volunteer to help you demonstrate how you want partners to turn their bodies at an angle and face each other as well as visually demonstrate specific expectations for active listening (eye contact, nods of understanding, etc.). You might then move into a live model of the talking part, letting the students listen in to the ways you are communicating with your partner. The better the model, the better your results will be.

Teaching can occur before, during, or after the modeling. When done before or during modeling, it can take the form of direct instruction about how to engage effectively in the Activator. It might sound like, "*When you turn to your partner I want you to make eye contact, so that your partner gets the signal you're tuning in to what they're saying.*" Teaching can also mean asking reflective questions to help students unpack the model for themselves. For example, after modeling how to communicate effectively with a partner in a Turn and Talk, a teacher might ask, "*What did you notice about the way we positioned ourselves? What did listening to a partner sound like/look like?*" In this way, students deconstruct what the teacher just demonstrated in order to "uncover" the expectations for the Activator. Teaching can also mean anticipating potential pitfalls students might encounter in the course of an Activator, for example, by clarifying that it is okay if partners do not agree with each other. Alternatively, teaching students how to maneuver around potential roadblocks might involve asking them to problem-solve beforehand. For example, a teacher might ask students to brainstorm some things they can do if their partner finishes speaking before the allotted time is up.

When you observe a skillful teacher preparing students to step into an Activator, the boundary between Teach and Model might be indiscernible. The next steps, **practice and assess**, should also be intertwined for optimal learning.

3. Practice and Assess

Activators require students to perform, and as with any performance, to do something flawlessly requires practice, practice, and more practice. Fortunately, **learning** is what takes place on the journey from being a novice to being able to deliver a skillful performance. So do not expect the performance or outcomes to be perfect initially, but do support students to ensure that learning is taking place within each round of practice. When you introduce a new Activator, be transparent with students that you are in "practice mode," stressing that you expect them to put in their full effort and get better at the Activator as time goes on. You could say, "*Given that this is the first time for us with this activity, I might need to pause the group at certain times to make sure we all know what to do so we can participate fully.*" You and your students will experience measures of success each time you try out an Activator—as long as you couple this practice with targeted feedback. This process can uncover gaps in skills and knowledge and provide an opportunity for students to reflect and grow. Soon you will observe increased levels of engagement in learning that permeates the rest of your lesson.

Occasionally you might encounter a student who is initially unwilling to participate. We suggest responding first by taking a moment to consider some of the reasons why. Often resistance is rooted in students feeling out of their comfort zone. Perhaps they are confused and need the question/prompt rephrased; perhaps they are uncomfortable speaking aloud to peers they do not know or they are not confident in their language proficiency; perhaps they are sleepy 16-year-olds who simply do not see the purpose in getting up when they just sat down. We know not to take it personally, and that we have to draw on expertise and try some different strategies to support engagement in the task.

Some important first steps with reluctant students would be to 1) clarify that the student understands the question or task, 2) acknowledge any feelings they might mention, 3) share with them what you hope they get out of it, and 4) make a polite, direct request that they be part of the experience. In a neutral voice you might say, *"What questions do you have about how to do the Activator? Ah, so you don't want to do this because you feel it is stupid? Well, please know that I appreciate the smart thinking you bring to class discussions."* (Or choose some other appreciative comment.) *"In my last period, the 10 minutes we spent on this activity really helped everyone understand the concepts we need to know in order to complete the unit project, so I am asking you to give it a try."*

Since practice is essential for success, it is important to get every student to participate as much as possible. Some students might resist until they see it in action a few times; possibly you will have a student or two who need time and additional one-to-one conversations with you to build trust before they participate fully. In some cases giving a student permission to observe the first time around can go a long way.

We want to emphasize the wisdom in going slow to go fast. During initial practice with an Activator, it will pay off to slow down each step and scaffold each component. The first time you do a particular Activator, you might have students practice it for a longer period of time (15 minutes instead seven minutes) or have them share with two partners instead of just one. When coupled with teacher persistence, before long this initial time investment will pay off in students' skillful engagement and deepened learning.

It is during these initial practice moments that you will need to artfully assess and provide feedback. While assessment is often narrowly defined as grading or testing, when we use the term assess or formative assessment, we are referring to providing feedback for learning (Shute, 2008). Constructive feedback is not communicated by giving a grade; instead, it is a targeted question or comment that supports students to reflect and self-correct in the moment until they meet the objective. It helps learners know in what ways their performance during a particular Activator is on track, in what ways it might be off track and what they need to do next. Feedback is essential during the early stages of acquiring any new skill in order to make sure the learner (as well as the group of learners) meets the learning outcome. Since the alternative is getting it wrong, we can't stress enough the importance of this component (Jones, 2010). And while some teachers might eventually incorporate Activators into a student participation grade, when feedback is given to guide students rather than evaluate their performance, it helps them embrace a learning stance around developing their competence rather than focus on doing the Activator just to get a good grade (Shute, 2008).

On the day you introduce an Activator, be prepared to constantly circulate around the room, intervening with individuals and groups to provide additional support and guidance. Above all, hold and communicate high expectations for students to put in their best efforts to think, share, and learn. We recommend starting with the Turn and Talk (additional detailed instructions on the Turn and Talk Activator can be found in Chapter 4).

3

The first time you have students practice a Turn and Talk, you may notice that one pair across the room—let's call them James and Maria—are not talking. While maintaining an eye on the whole group, you immediately make your way over to them so you can quietly clarify the expectations: "*During a Turn and Talk partners need to be talking the entire two minutes, or you can raise your hand if you need to ask me a question.*" You might give some suggestions for how to keep the conversation going: "*If you and your partner are not sure what to say, you can take turns asking questions about the prompt instead of just responding to it but no matter what, I should see and hear a conversation for the full two minutes. Are you good to go? Great. Talk away.*"

Feedback that praises and draws attention to effort and on-track behavior is equally important and has an impact on student achievement. (Dean et al., 2012) Highlighting an individual or a group's exemplary behavior cues them to feel their success. This impacts their future effort, which results in an increased occurrence of that exemplary behavior. In other words, make sure to take advantage of any opportunity to leverage strengths. For example, after the two minutes of the Turn and Talk, you could share with the whole group that James and Maria initially did not feel like they had a lot to talk about, so they started asking questions about the prompt. "*I heard some really smart questions. Let me share one: 'I wonder if this question somehow connects to what we learned about the history of Afghanistan last week?' What an insightful question. Our goal is that we all think, share, and learn during Turn and Talks. I encourage all of you to consider asking questions if you and your partner experience a lull in your conversation the next time we do a Turn and Talk.*" This kind of teacher talk is effective because it is asset based, normalizes a challenge, celebrates effort, and clarifies expectations.

Much of the learning will hinge upon a thoughtful debrief. This is where students will reflect on their experience during the Activator and get corrective feedback on the content knowledge in order to confirm, refine, or restructure their understanding. To have the greatest impact on achievement, it is important to ask both content-based debrief questions and process-based debrief questions to support students' metacognition about what they learned, how they learned, and what they need to do next (Hattie & Timperley, 2007). For example, you might first ask, (content) "*What are some of the things you learned about trench warfare in World War I?*" and follow up with (process) "*What are some ways that working in groups at Rotation Stations supported you with learning the information?*" In some cases it might make sense to focus on the content first and then debrief the process. In other situations you might need to let students talk about the process before they are able to reflect on the substance of the Activator.

You will be working hard the day you introduce a new Activator, and likely the next few times as students find their way to meet the expectations of the new format. It will be critical to be clear about your expectations, confident in your facilitation, strategic about your debrief questions, and intentional in your feedback to ensure a high level of engagement from your students. The payoff is watching your students engage emotionally, cognitively, and behaviorally. With practice, your group will hear the words Turn and Talk and know immediately what to do and how to be successful.

Exploring the Activators

Each of the Activators described in Chapters 4-17 contains three key elements: detailed facilitation instructions, suggestions for using the Activator to create a High-Performing Community of Learners, and specific examples for using the Activator in core content areas to support various instructional purposes. We encourage our readers to visit each chapter, tune into the directions and effective facilitation tips, explore the content examples, and consider how you might incorporate each Activator into your instruction over the course of the year. While we know not every Activator is a perfect fit for each subject or every teacher, it is our hope that this book becomes one of your primary resources for student engagement and that the pages become dog-eared with wear.

3

> *In this era of standardization and the Common Core, the practice of elevating student voice might seem countercultural, but given the importance of agency, autonomy and self-regulation in student learning, it is really rather commonsensical.*
>
> —Eric Toshalis and Michael J. Nakkula

Foundational Activators

This chapter offers three foundational Activators that quickly increase student voice, require little preparation on the teacher's part, and are relatively straightforward to facilitate: **Turn and Talk**, **Popcorn**, and **Wave**. Their elegant simplicity belie their power to increase engagement in learning, and regular practice with Turn and Talk, Popcorn, and Wave prepares students to step into more complex Activators found in later chapters. Consistent use of these Activators puts student voice front and center and creates a High-Performing Community of Learners who are confident and comfortable to share their thoughts and who value multiple perspectives.

How do Foundational Activators support the conditions for engagement?

- Garner **good will** by acknowledging and welcoming multiple perspectives
- Support **participation** by creating a platform for everyone's voice
- Capture **attention** by providing an audience of peers
- Increase **interest** by injecting relevance
- Foster **effort** by providing a forum for trying out ideas
- Support **investment** by making room for students to reflect on Classroom Expectations and ClassroomAgreements

Turn and Talk

All students respond to a prompt by turning and sharing their thinking with a partner.

A Turn and Talk—also referred to as Think-Pair-Share (Lyman, 1981)—is an essential tool for constructing a well-paced lesson that gets everyone's voice in the room quickly. Since each student is expected to think and participate, this Activator ramps up accountability as well as engagement. Because it is a component of several other Activators, there is a big payoff in helping students become skilled at Turn and Talks right from the start. Key to success with this Activator is designing engaging prompts.

TIME: 2–5 MINUTES

TEACHER PREP LIST:

- ❑ Design an engaging prompt aligned with a learning outcome
- ❑ Identify a different prompt for modeling and a student volunteer to help model the Activator
- ❑ Display prompt and student directions
- ❑ Timer

STUDENT DIRECTIONS

1. Do a Quick Jot in response to the prompt.

2. Share your response with your partner.

3. Ask questions or make connections to your partner's response.

SET UP THE ACTIVATOR

1. Explain the purpose of the Activator. You might say, "*We are going to do a Turn and Talk Activator, which will give you a chance to explore your thinking about _____ with one other classmate. Listening carefully to your partner will help you check in on your own thinking and may even give you some new ideas. Afterwards, I'll ask some of you to share highlights of your conversation with the rest of the group.*"

2. Review student directions.

3. Tell students they will talk about a prompt with a partner for one minute. Indicate which students are paired together.

MODEL AND TEACH

1. Arrange two desks in the front of the room that are angled towards each other. Ask for a volunteer to model the Turn and Talk with you. Make eye contact with your partner.

2. Show a sample prompt on the board.

3. Emphasize that students do not have to agree on their responses; the goal is to explore their thinking with a partner.

4. Invite your partner to respond first. Listen attentively (make eye contact, nod, smile, etc.) Respond by asking a question or making a connection to what your partner said.

5. Share your response to the prompt.

6. Ask students what they noticed about what you and your partner did during the Turn and Talk (angled your bodies towards each other, made eye contact, took turns talking, asked questions, made connections)

7. Remind students that Classroom Expectations and Classroom Agreements apply to all types of classroom conversations, including Turn and Talks.

PRACTICE AND ASSESS

1. Direct students to the displayed prompt and ask them to jot down a response.

2. Offer words of encouragement and let students know you're excited to hear their thinking. Circulate, monitor, and support students, as needed.

3. Announce when time is halfway up and when there are a few seconds remaining.

4. Use a signal to get the group's attention and ask a few students to share "headlines" from their Turn and Talks.

5. Debrief by asking a few of the following content and process questions:

Content Questions

- What are some ways you're thinking about _____ ?
- Was your response the same or different than your partner's?
- What are some things you learned about _____ ?
- What are some things you're still wondering about _____ ?

Process Questions

- What was it like to share your thinking with a partner?
- Did the amount of time feel too long? Too short? Just right?

Thank students for their active participation, affirm understandings, and address any misconceptions that surfaced.

TROUBLESHOOTING TIPS

1. If there is an uneven number of students, make a trio. While the third person in the trio is sharing, invite pairs to ask each other questions about what they said earlier.

2. If you notice a pair that is not talking, move to these students, clarify expectations, and ask students what they might do to keep the conversation going. If students need some help, you might offer a suggestion, for example, asking each other questions.

VARIATIONS AND EXTENSIONS

1. When introducing Turn and Talk, you might want to support students' capacity to speak and listen effectively by structuring the conversation. Ask each participant to decide if they are "A" or "B." The "A's" speak for 30 seconds while the "B's" listen in engaged silence (eye contact, nodding head, etc.). At the signal, students switch roles and the "B's" respond to the same prompt while the "A's" listen in engaged silence.

2. Have students ask a question or paraphrase what their partners said.

Popcorn

Without raising hands, multiple students respond to a prompt with a brief thought or idea in random order.

A Popcorn Activator generates momentum in a lesson by getting a variety of perspectives in the room in a short amount of time. The informal, random-order sharing keeps students on their toes, creates curiosity, and promotes active listening. And the silence in between the words allows students to reflect, rehearse, and make connections.

TIME: 3-5 MINUTES

TEACHER PREP LIST:

❑ Design an engaging prompt linked to a learning outcome

❑ Display prompt and student directions

❑ Timer

STUDENT DIRECTIONS

1. Do a Quick Jot in response to the prompt.

2. When the signal is given, share out your response without raising your hand.

3. If two or more people speak at once, pause, make eye contact and decide who will go first, then share in that order.

4. When there is a pause, reflect on the previous speaker's words, make connections to your response or rehearse your thinking.

5. Listen attentively to others.

SET UP THE ACTIVATOR

1. Explain the purpose of the Activator. You might say, "*We're going to a do a Popcorn Activator so we can hear what different classmates think about Thank you for staying on your toes and listening carefully since we're going to respond without raising hands for _____ minutes.*"

2. Review student directions. Explain that students will respond to the prompt in random order without raising hands. Make a connection to the Activator's name – just as popcorn kernels pop in random order, so will students' responses pop up around the room. Emphasize that the silence in between responses is equally important, since it allows everyone to process what has been said and to build on previous ideas. Explain that each student will have the opportunity to respond once before anyone responds a second time.

MODEL AND TEACH

1. Model with a sample prompt for a shorter amount of time. For example, "*Let's try it with this easy question: What is your favorite kind of pizza? Let me hear three responses. 'Cheese.' 'Pepperoni.' 'Giardano's because they have the best crust.' Good. That is how Popcorn works.*"

2. Emphasize that repeated responses are okay and can even highlight important ideas for the group.

3. Remind students of relevant Classroom Expectations or Classroom Agreements.

4. Emphasize that when students "popcorn" responses, they chime in, build off of each other's comments, and set the pace rather than raising their hands or having the teacher call on individuals.

PRACTICE AND ASSESS

1. Direct students to the prompt on the board, and give them time to jot down a response.

2. Tell students they will "popcorn" responses as a whole group for three minutes.

3. Express your confidence that you will hear a variety of thoughtful responses.

4. Invite responses by saying, *"Begin"* or *"The floor is open."*

5. Let students know when there is one minute remaining.

6. Use a signal to get the group's attention, and debrief by asking some of the following content and process questions:

Content Questions
- What are some things you heard that stood out to you?
- What patterns did you notice in the responses?
- What are some things you realized or are wondering about _____ ?

Process Questions
- What was it like to participate in this Activator?
- What did you find yourself thinking or doing during this Activator?

Thank students for their participation, affirm understandings, and address any misconceptions that may have surfaced.

4

TROUBLESHOOTING TIPS

1. If students are reluctant to share, precede this Activator with a Turn and Talk so students have an opportunity to rehearse their ideas.

2. If students are challenged by speaking in random order without raising hands, ask them to raise hands. Call on the first person and then put the students in charge. After the first speaker responds, s/he calls on the next student whose hand is raised. Continue until all students who have raised their hands have had an opportunity to speak. Students will have to know each other's names in order to do this with ease and efficiency.

3. If you do this Activator in the middle or end of a class in which participation has been uneven, consider asking students who haven't participated in the last 10 minutes, to be sure to share.

4. If students are racing through the Activator without appreciating the silence in between responses, ask them to consider the benefits of allowing some silence in between responses.

VARIATIONS AND EXTENSIONS

1. Ask students to do a Quick Jot before or after the Popcorn Activator.

2. If done at the end of class, you might couple it with an Exit Ticket*.

Wave

All students respond to a prompt in rapid order with a single word or phrase.

This Activator is a very quick way of collecting a response from everyone in the room. A Wave injects a jolt of energy into a lesson's pacing, since students respond to a prompt in rapid succession with just a word or phrase. The speed of responding coupled with the challenge of distilling ideas down to just a few essential words captures students' attention and packs this Activator with intellectual rigor.

TIME: 1–3 MINUTES

TEACHER PREP LIST

- ❑ Design an engaging prompt aligned with a learning outcome that can be answered succinctly with a word or phrase.
- ❑ Display prompt and student directions.
- ❑ Timer

STUDENT DIRECTIONS

1. Take a few moments to think about your response.
2. Be mindful of the speaking order and listen attentively to each response.
3. Share your word/phrase when it is your turn.

SET UP THE ACTIVATOR

1. Explain the purpose of the Activator. You might say, "We're going to do a Wave Activator so we can hear everyone's smart ideas about _____ really quickly. I'm going to challenge you to respond in just a few words and stay on your toes, so we can move around the room to hear all your responses in two minutes."
2. Review student directions.
3. Emphasize that responses are limited to a word or phrase.
4. Remind students of any relevant Classroom Expectations or Classroom Agreements.

MODEL AND TEACH

1. Ask for a volunteer to start the Wave and be explicit about the order in which students will respond, for example, "Chris will start us off and then it will be Jessica, Xavier, Danielle, etc."
2. Show a sample prompt and model how students might respond in the designated order: "My favorite ice cream flavor is vanilla (point to Chris) chocolate fudge (point to Jessica), mint chocolate chip (point to Xavier), vanilla (point to Danielle), etc."

3. Explain that students can say "pass" if they are not ready to go. Tell them you will give them another opportunity at the end.

4. Emphasize that completing the prompt the same way someone else did is okay; in fact, it might mean that this is an important idea worth paying attention to.

PRACTICE AND ASSESS

1. Display the prompt, and give everyone a few moments of think time to consider their responses.

2. Say, "*Begin*", and point to students to indicate the speaking order, as needed.

3. At the end, go back and invite any student who might have passed earlier to respond by asking, "*Is there anything you might want to add?*"

4. Debrief by asking some of the following content and process questions:

Content Questions
■ What are some things that stood out to you?
■ What patterns did you notice in the responses?
■ What did you realize or what are you wondering about _____ ?

Process Questions
■ What was it like to participate in this Activator?
■ In what ways was it easy or challenging?

Thank students for their participation, affirm understandings, and address any misconceptions that may have surfaced.

TROUBLESHOOTING TIPS

1. If the Wave gets stalled because students are confused about the order, stop and review the sequence and start again.

2. If students are struggling to drill their response down to a word or phrase, ask them to do a Quick Jot first. Then tell them to go back and circle a word or phrase that gets at the heart of what they're saying.

VARIATIONS AND EXTENSIONS

1. Chart patterns of responses as well as any surprises or wonderings. Explore these further through a Turn and Talk and/or a whole-group discussion.

2. If you do the Wave Activator at the end of class, you might ask students to write their response on sticky notes and to put these up on a designated wall space on their way out. Use these in your next class to build a bridge from the previous to the current lesson.

3. Have students write a paragraph explaining the word/phrase they selected. When appropriate, ask them to use textual evidence to support their thinking.

4. Take notes during the Wave and type up some of the responses. Project them the next day and ask students to explore some of these further using another Activator format like the Mix and Mingle Activator (Chapter 17).

Create a High-Performing Community of Learners

Trust is critical to creating a High-Performing Community of Learners since many young people need to know that teachers care for them as individuals before they will learn from us. We understand it can be challenging to find time and opportunities for this when there are many students in a class. That's where Foundational Activators come in—their formats provide teachers with quick ways to check in with each student. For example, acknowledging young peoples' feelings about your subject with a quick Popcorn or Wave prompt like, *"A word to describe how I feel about _____ "* (content area) communicates that you care about students' feelings and past experiences with your subject. Investing in building Trust and Belonging through these quick Activators brings a big payoff. Students get the message that your classroom is a safe place to learn, which is essential to creating a High-Performing Community of Learners.

For more information on the issue of respect among and between students and teachers, please see Carol Miller Lieber's *Getting Classroom Management Right: Guided Discipline and Personalized Support in Secondary Schools*, page 104 (Educators for Social Responsibility, 2009).

Foundational Activators offer vehicles for establishing Classroom Expectations and ClassroomAgreements that anchor a High-Performing Community of Learners. When designing theseClassroom Agreements, students will often use the word "respect." Because this is a word that is abstract and often means different things to different people, it is essential that students name very concrete behaviors that show (through words and actions) how to treat someone with respect. Asking students to engage in a Turn and Talk or Popcorn Activator in response to the following prompt can unpack this word: *"If I had a movie camera here in the classroom, what behaviors would I film that would show you treating each other with respect?"* Afterwards, the group can use their responses to formulate Classroom Agreements that will help them take ownership and exercise accountability around respectful behaviors they commit to using.

Foundational Activators are also tools for reinforcing Habits of Learning. Prior to filling out a self-assessment at the end of the week or unit, students might engage in a Turn and Talk to reflect on one Habit of Learning they have made the most progress with. This provides students an opportunity to process their ideas before filling out the self-reflection form, holds them accountable to a classmate, and creates a High-Performing Community of Learners that honors effort and encourages metacognition.

Using Foundational Activators for Creating a High-Performing Community of Learners

- Turn and Talk: Which agreement is hardest for the group to keep? What are some things we can do to help everyone get better at keeping this agreement?
- Turn and Talk: Who is an adult you consider successful? What are some things that make this adult successful?
- Turn and Talk: What Habit of Learning have you made big improvements in? What are some things that have helped you make improvements?

- Popcorn/Wave: One thing I still need to complete, revise or redo is _____ .
- Popcorn/Wave: If I had a movie camera here in the classroom, what behaviors would I film that would show you treating each other with respect?
- Popcorn/Wave: A word or phrase I might hear indicating that we're living up to our Classroom Agreements is _____ .
- Popcorn/Wave: A word to describe how I feel about (subject area) is _____ .

Using Foundational Activators to Support Learning in the Content Areas

Generate Connections to Prior Knowledge: Foundational Activators can enlist adolescents' interest and activate prior knowledge prior to reading in any course. In a ninth grade biology unit on the food chain, students might make predictions about the provocatively entitled article, "Sea Otter Fights Global Warming." This type of prompt ramps up students' curiosity about what they'll encounter in the text while inviting them to draw on what they've previously learned about the carbon cycle. Making independent predictions and sharing these with a partner prior to reading propels adolescents' movement through a text in order to "test" which predictions will be proven accurate.

Provide Opportunities for Practicing Skills and Deepening Understanding: Foundational Activators are critical for providing all students opportunities for mastering content and strengthening skills, especially in large classes. When there are many students in an algebra class, inserting a Turn and Talk in which students analyze the degree of a polynomial function supports everyone in thinking through a challenge, not just the one student who raises her hand or who is asked to go up to the board. By ritualizing the use of Foundational Activators around unit learning outcomes, an algebra teacher can offer the repeated practice necessary for all learners to hone skills and achieve learning outcomes.

Provide Opportunities for Formative Assessment: Popcorn Activators are ideal for quickly getting a read of the room in terms of what students know and can do. English language arts teachers often support understanding of literary elements and summarizing skills by asking students to summarize the reading of fictional texts using a Somebody (character) / Wanted (goal/objective) / But (conflict) / So (resolution) framework. Students who share their summaries using a Popcorn Activator provide important feedback for the teacher. Hearing multiple summaries also injects creative tension into the classroom as students encounter divergent ideas that encourage them to re-evaluate their own. Afterwards, the teacher might ask students to assess what summaries get at the heart of a chapter's conflict. Alternatively, if the Popcorn Activator revealed students' need for further support in constructing a summary, she might decide to conduct an on-the-spot mini-lesson for this purpose.

Prepare Students for Assessments: Prior to an end-of-course world history final assessment, a Wave Activator might be used to quickly collect a variety of responses to the prompt, "*Name a technological development that changed the world.*" Hearing multiple answers will jog students' memories and provide a jumping off point for students to select and elaborate on two or three of these responses in their study guides.

Inject Relevance Into the Curriculum: Since foundational Activators quickly fill a classroom with student voice, they are a relatively easy way of making content more immediate for adolescents. As students learn basic vocabulary that might be used in an "Introducing Ourselves" unit, a world language teacher might insert a Wave into a lesson where students share their birthdays, favorite colors, or one thing they like to do in their free time. Having the chance to talk about themselves and to find out about their peers captures young people's attention and increases their capacity to remember the new vocabulary.

Math

Algebra

Turn and Talk/Popcorn: What is the degree of this polynomial function? What are some other possibilities?

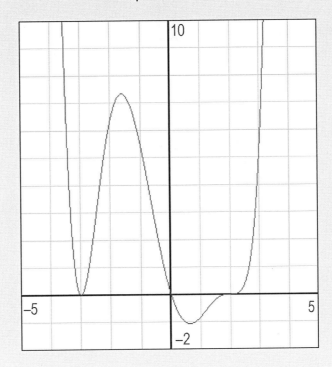

Geometry

Turn and Talk/Popcorn: Both Jessie and Tami are given the triangle shown below and are asked to find the length of c. Jessie says that c = 31 while Tami says that c = 25. Who is correct? Explain completely and identify the error that lead to the incorrect answer.

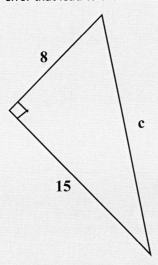

Science

Earth Science

Turn and Talk/Popcorn: What are some ways you might describe the relationship between rocks and minerals?

Popcorn/Wave: A word/phrase that gets at the heart of plate tectonics is _____ .

Biology

Turn and Talk/Popcorn: Based upon what you know about the Food Chain, what predictions might you make about how "Sea Otters Fight Global Warming" as described in the article?

Popcorn/Wave: When you hear Darwin's Theory of Evolution, what comes to mind?

Chemistry

Turn and Talk: What chemical element would you most like to be? Provide two to three reasons to support your answer.

Popcorn/Wave: What is one thing you learned about the quantum mechanical model?

Physics

Turn and Talk: Describe some examples of state change.

Popcorn/Wave: What do you think of when you hear the word "energy?"

Social Studies

U.S. History

Turn and Talk: What are some differences between the way the U.S. Civil War was fought and the ways civil wars are fought today? To what extent are there any similarities?

Popcorn/Wave: Name one of the New Deal programs.

World History

Turn and Talk: What role did the river play in early civilizations?

Popcorn/Wave: Name a technological development that changed the world.

Government

Turn and Talk: What are some reasons you think the Media is often referred to as the fourth branch of government?

Popcorn/Wave: What are some things the U.S. government "regulates?"

Economics

Turn and Talk: What are some of the economic impacts NAFTA had on the U.S., Mexico, and Canada?

Popcorn/Wave: What is one way your life has been impacted by globalization? What is one way it will continue to be impacted by an increasingly interconnected world?

English Language Arts

Writing

Turn and Talk: What are some strengths of the sample essay? What are some things you might suggest the writer focus on in the next draft?

Popcorn/Wave: What is a sensory detail you used in order to create an image for your readers?

Reading – Literature

Turn and Talk: What are some ways that Gogol tries to remake his identity in the novel *The Namesake?*

Popcorn/Wave: Share your sentence summary of Chapter 4 of *Roll of Thunder, Hear My Cry* using the Somebody/Wanted/But/So framework.

Reading – Informational Texts

Turn and Talk: What are some ways that the text answers the essential question, " _____ ?"

Popcorn/Wave: A headline of five words or less that captures a key idea in _____ .

Speaking and Listening

Turn and Talk: Identify a type of rhetoric the speaker used and the impact it had on you as a listener.

Popcorn/Wave: What is a question you might offer to jumpstart our conversation about _____ ?

Language

Turn and Talk: What are some ways of changing the following sentence to make it gender neutral? "If a student studies hard, he will succeed."

Popcorn/Wave: What are some examples of subjective writing?

World Languages

Turn and Talk: Partner A, pretend to be a waiter and ask your partner in (the target language) what they would like to eat. Partner B, respond with your order in (the target language). Switch roles and repeat.

Turn and Talk: Turn to your partner and share the vocabulary words that have been challenging for you to remember.

Popcorn/Wave: If you could visit any city in the world where (target language) is spoken, where would you go and why?

Popcorn/Wave: What is your favorite color?

Popcorn/Wave: What is your favorite season?

Popcorn/Wave: When is your birthday?

Popcorn/Wave: What is your favorite thing to do in your free time?

Suggestions for Writing Your Own Turn and Talk and Popcorn Activators:

Think about one of your upcoming lessons and consider where you might insert a Turn and Talk to support pacing of the lesson and help students construct meaning around the learning outcome. Another idea is to bookend your week on Mondays and Fridays with one of these formats to create a High-Performing Community of Learners.

Your Turn

Design Your Own Foundational Activators

A Checklist for Designing Effective Activators:

☐ *Does the prompt support a specific learning outcome?*

☐ *Is the prompt engaging?* Can students respond without feeling anxious or uncomfortable? Do students have enough prior knowledge to feel competent in their responses? Will the prompt ignite curiosity, make content relevant, and challenge students to think at a high level?

☐ *Is the prompt crafted with invitational language that promotes exploration and reduces the need for certainty?* Invitational prompts might begin with "What might...?" "What are some of the...?" or "What is your hunch for why...?"

CHAPTER

---

*Simply put, students who feel respected and supported,
who feel seen, heard, known, and understood do better in school.*

—Educators for Social Responsibility (from *Getting Advisory Right*)

Activators to Kick-Start Your Year

Students learn each other's names, get to know
and feel known by their peers, and become accustomed to
the expectation of active and thoughtful participation.

A former colleague used to say, "You have to go slow to go fast later, or for that matter to go anywhere." His mantra captures the essence of why we feel so strongly about starting the year with Activators designed to create a High-Performing Community of Learners. As we continue to stress, when students feel safe and connected, they are ready to learn and engage and perform at higher levels (Becker & Luthar, 2002; Klem & Connell, 2004; Osher, Sprague, Weissburg, Axelrod, Keenan, Kendziora, & Zins 2008). With all the pressures teachers have to teach an ever-expanding curriculum, we understand the notion that there is "no time to waste" and we know that classroom culture is intricately tied to student achievement. Establishing the optimal classroom conditions is what gives you the time and opportunity for deep learning to occur. So while creating a High-Performing Community of Learners does require investing time at the start of the year to engage students in community-building Activators, we know it is an investment that will payoff tenfold in the months that follow.

Adolescents act and engage differently depending upon whether they feel known or anonymous. Each Activator in this chapter is designed to help students feel known, connect to the group, learn each other's names, communicate that you want to know them as individuals, and establish that you expect and value their active participation. All of these conditions are foundational for student engagement. Consider integrating three or more of these Activators during the first two weeks of school to kick-start the year.

The Activators we have included in this chapter are tried and true and include some of our favorites. For example, we can't imagine starting a school year without the Name Tent Toss. It not only helps us remember 90 percent of names by the end of the first day, but also provides an immediate dose of positive energy and enthusiasm. Your students will also have their favorites. We've had classes that insisted on doing the Weather Report every Monday, and classes that want to extend the Paired Interviews by continuing to have everyone respond to additional interesting questions each week. Don't be surprised if one of these becomes your favorite go-to Activator in years to come or takes on a life of its own with your students.

What are some ways these Activators support conditions for engagement?

- Garner **good will** by sending a signal that this is a safe place to learn at the beginning of the year.
- Support **participation** by developing belonging.
- Capture **attention** by injecting a dose of fun and energy into the classroom.
- Increase **interest** by providing relevance, challenge, novelty, and surprise.

Activators to Create a High-Performing Community of Learners at the Beginning of the Year:

Name Tent Toss

Name and Motion

"You Name It" Line-Ups

Paired Interviews

Common Ground

Weather Report

Color Chips

Name Tent Toss

TEACHER PREP LIST

- ❑ Make a model name tent
- ❑ Display student directions
- ❑ Display questions students will answer on inside of name tent
- ❑ Cardstock (cut in half to save paper)
- ❑ Markers
- ❑ Timer
- ❑ Identify a space where students can circle up (standing)
- ❑ Box or bucket (optional)

STUDENT DIRECTIONS

1. Make a name tent with your first and last name in large letters.

2. Jot down responses to the posted questions on the inside of your name tent.

3. Hold up your name tent and say your name and your response to **one** of the questions.

4. Toss your name tent into the middle of the circle.

5. Volunteers call out names and return name tents to each person.

SET UP THE ACTIVATOR

1. Explain the purpose of the Activator. You might say, "*We're going to do an Activator to learn names and find out a little bit about each other. What are some reasons knowing names might be helpful? The challenge and movement in this Activator will help our brains remember the names more easily.*"

2. Distribute one piece (or half-piece) of cardstock to each student and ask students to fold it in half the long way or "like a hotdog" to create a name tent. Let students know that these name tents will be used for the first few weeks of school to help everyone get to know each other's names.

Name Tent Toss

Name Tent Example

MODEL AND TEACH

1. Show a model of how you would like the name tent to be completed. We recommend having students write their first and last name using a marker and writing in clear large print in the center of the name tent.

2. Using a pen or a pencil, have students jot a word, a phrase, or an image inside the name tent to represent their responses to two or three low-risk questions such as: *"What is a food you can't live without? What is a subject in school where you feel like you have learned things that will help you in life? What's a movie you would want to see again? What is something you like to do in your free time?"*

3. Distribute a marker to each student and give them a few minutes to complete the outside and inside of their name tents.

4. As soon as students are ready, have them stand and form a circle and hold their name tent up in front of their waist so that everyone can see their face and their name tent. Include yourself in the circle and model exactly how you would like them to hold the name tent.

5. Let students know that they will be asked to say their name and then share one of their responses from the inside of their name tent. For example: *"I'm _____ and I couldn't live without Italian food because I love pasta."*

6. Model for students by going first. Give them 20 seconds of think time to decide what they want to share from the inside of their name tent; ask for a volunteer to begin and then let the class know you will proceed clockwise around the circle.

5

PRACTICE AND ASSESS

1. When all students have had a chance to introduce themselves and share a "favorite," ask them to toss their name tent gently into the center of the circle. Alternatively, if you don't have empty space in the middle of your circle you could have them put their name tent in a box or a bucket in the center of the room and then return to the circle.

2. Ask for two volunteers to go into the middle of the circle (or to the box or bucket) and return all name tents by **calling out the name** on each name tent and then returning it to the right person as quickly as possible. Stop and remind students if they are not calling out names or not saying them loud enough. The more students hear names said aloud the easier it will be for them to remember names. Hearing their own name said aloud numerous times will also increase each student's feelings of being "known" by their classmates.

3. Explain that this is an exercise about making everyone feel welcome, so if someone has trouble remembering or pronouncing a name, others around the circle will offer hints or help. Encourage and model how to help the volunteers in the middle by directing them to the right student when they need help. For example, *"Julia is behind you in the red shirt!"*

4. Secretly time how long it takes for the first volunteers to return all name tents.

5. Announce how long it took for the first volunteers to return all the name tents and thank them for participating (this is where you can introduce applause when honoring effort). Now ask for a second pair of volunteers to try to beat the first pair's time. Have all participants toss their name tents into the circle or box/bucket and repeat the exercise.

6. Announce the second pair's time and thank everyone for their participation.

7. Be sure to collect name tents at the end of the class so you have them for students to put on their desk during the first two weeks of school. Consider designating a spot on a bookshelf for each class to stack their name tents.

8. Debrief by asking some of the following questions: *"What was it like to do this Activator? What was easy? What was challenging? In what ways can learning names help us work and learn together?"*

Thank students for their active participation.

Name and Motion

TIME: 15-20 MINUTES

TEACHER PREP LIST
❏ Identify a space where students can circle up (either standing or with their desks)

❏ Display student directions

STUDENT DIRECTIONS
1. Think about something you love to do and a gesture or motion that represents this.

2. Repeat the names of the three previous students as well as the motions that represent what they love to do.

3. Say your name and make a motion that represents something you love to do.

SET UP THE ACTIVATOR
1. Explain the purpose of the Activator. You might say, *"We're going to do an Activator to learn names and find out a little bit about each other. What are some reasons we might spend time getting to know each other's names? I realize this Activator might feel a little weird at first—that's okay since I'm confident the 'strangeness' is going to help us all remember the names more easily. Thanks for giving it a try."*

2. Have the group form a circle by standing.

3. Review student directions.

MODEL AND TEACH

1. Ask students to think about something they love to do, as well as a gesture or motion that represents this activity. Front-load your expectation about the motions that students select. You might say, *"And just to be clear—motions need to be appropriate, so if you are going to show your latest dance move it needs to be PG."* Model with your name and a motion of your own. Example: *"I'm Ms. Allen and I like to cook"* (teacher models stirring a pot).

2. Tell students that they will repeat the names and motions of the three previous people before they say their name and make their own gesture. Ask the student to your left to begin. Model by repeating this student's name and do his/her motion before saying your name and making your gesture. Example: *"This is Isabella and she likes to sing"* (holds imaginary microphone). *"I'm Ms. Allen and I like to cook"* (stirs a pot).

PRACTICE AND ASSESS

1. Proceed around the circle until every student has an opportunity to share his/her name and gesture and to repeat those of the previous three students.

2. If students can't recall a name or gesture, invite them to ask classmates to repeat names or motions, so they can say/do them. Afterwards, thank them for the opportunity to hear the name or see the motion again.

3. Notice if some students might be uncomfortable making the gesture and encourage them to say what the gesture represents instead.

4. Debrief by asking some of the following questions: *"What was it like to do this Activator? Any surprises? What is one thing you have in common with someone in the class? What are some of the things this group has in common?"*

Thank students for their active participation.

"You Name It" Line-Ups

TIME: 5-10 MINUTES

TEACHER PREP LIST

❑ Identify a space where students can stand in a straight line, "U," circle, or square.

❑ Display student directions.

❑ Timer

STUDENT DIRECTIONS

1. Think about the **first** letter of your **first** name and where it falls in the alphabet.

2. Move to the section of the line that represents where your name falls alphabetically.

3. Communicate in silence (using gestures and body language) to find your position in the line.

SET UP THE ACTIVATOR

1. Explain the purpose of this Activator. You might say, *"We're going to do an Activator that will help us understand how we're doing with learning names."*

2. Review student directions.

3. Have students predict how long it might take for the group to line up silently in alphabetical order by first name.

MODEL AND TEACH

1. Ask students to line up **silently** (ranging from A on left and Z on the extreme right). If there is not enough space to make a straight line, a "U," circle, square or any similar shape will work.

2. Model how to do this with an example. You might say, *"So if my name were 'Sabrina,' I would move to the second half of the line, since 'S' is in the second half of the alphabet, a few letters after 'M.' Then I'd use gestures to communicate and try to figure out my exact position in the line."*

PRACTICE AND ASSESS

1. Ask students to begin. Circulate and monitor that students are communicating silently. Use body/sign language to support any students who might need assistance.

2. Once the class has lined up, ask students if they are confident about their positions. If not, give them another 30 seconds to check in with their neighbors silently.

3. When students are ready, ask them to go down the line and say their names. If students positioned themselves incorrectly, invite them to move into the correct order.

4. Debrief by asking a few of the following questions: *"What did you notice happened during the Activator? How did we do with our prediction? Any surprises? If we were to do this Activator again next week, what goal would you like to set for how long it will take us? What additional strategies might we use to decrease the time?"*

5. Thank students for their active participation.

VARIATIONS AND EXTENSIONS

Students can say the first letter of the word they are using to line themselves up according to:

- Birthday (January on the left and December all the way to the right)
- The first letter of a future career (A on the left and Z all the way to the right)
- The first letter of something they are looking forward to doing over the winter break (A on the left and Z all the way to the right)
- The first letter of something they could teach someone else to do (A on the left and Z all the way to the right)

Paired Interviews

This Activator takes a little more time than the others but it is worth the investment, since everyone immediately feels known by one other person in the room.

TIME: 20-25 MINUTES

5

TEACHER PREP LIST

- ❏ Design suggested student interview questions
- ❏ Display suggested student interview questions and student directions
- ❏ Decide on how to group students so they will interview someone they don't know
- ❏ Paper and pens/pencils (optional)

STUDENT DIRECTIONS

1. Choose three questions you will use to interview a partner.
2. Sit next to your partner and make eye contact.
3. Take turns asking each other questions, and provide details in your responses.
4. Communicate that you're listening through body language.
5. Thank your partner and ask permission to share one thing you learned with the class.

SET UP THE ACTIVATOR

1. Explain the purpose of the Activator. You might say, *"I expect this to be a classroom community where you learn as much from each other as you do from me, so it's important that you start to get to know each other a little bit. This Paired Interview Activator we're about to do is a way to do this."*
2. Review student directions.
3. Draw students' attention to some sample questions that students can use. Elicit a few additional questions students might consider asking and write these on the board.

4. Ask students to select three questions they would like to ask a partner.

5. Pair students up.

MODEL AND TEACH

1. Ask a volunteer to model the Activator with you.

2. Model how to sit with your partner by positioning your desks side by side and at an angle, so you can make eye contact with each other.

3. Model asking a question of your partner and responding to a question.

4. Debrief by asking students what they noticed about how you interviewed (you smiled, nodded, avoided interrupting, asked follow-up questions etc.) and responded to your partner (you elaborated and provided details).

PRACTICE AND ASSESS

1. Give pairs four to five minutes to ask each other three questions.

2. Circulate and monitor that students are engaging in on-task conversations.

3. Support students who have finished early by asking, "*What are some things you learned about your partner? What are some things you might still want to find out?*" Encourage them to continue their interviews using some of these questions.

4. Remind students when time is halfway up.

5. Use a signal to get the group's attention, and ask students to thank their partners and ask permission regarding one thing they learned that they would like to share with the class.

6. Invite students to share one thing they learned about their partners.

7. Debrief by asking some of the following questions: "*What was it like to conduct a peer interview? What did you realize? Any surprises?*"

Thank students for their active participation.

SOME SUGGESTED INTERVIEW QUESTIONS:

1. What's the best thing about being a teenager? The hardest?

2. What is a TV show or movie you could watch over and over? Why?

3. If you could spend 24 hours with one famous person, dead or alive, who would it be? Why?

4. Name one thing you could teach someone how to make or do.

5. What is a holiday you and your family celebrate and what is one tradition you have to celebrate it?

VARIATIONS AND EXTENSIONS

Give out index cards and ask students to jot down notes in response to the questions they ask. Collect these and use the information to make personal connections with students when appropriate and possible, for example, when you meet and greet them at the door, *"So your favorite TV show is _____ ? I really like the lead actress."* You might also let students know you will collect the cards and read out a few responses each day to see if the class can guess whose answers they are.

Common Ground

TIME: 10-15 MINUTES

TEACHER PREP LIST:

- ❏ Scrap paper (one piece per group)
- ❏ Pens (one per group)
- ❏ Timer
- ❏ Display student directions and a list of possible categories of what students have in common
- ❏ Decide on how you will group students

STUDENT DIRECTIONS

1. Select a student to be the recorder for your group.

2. Make a list of things *all* your group members have in common.

SET UP THE ACTIVATOR

1. Explain the purpose of the activity. You might say, *"The Activator we're going to do will help you figure out what you have in common with some of your classmates. This can help you be more comfortable working and learning from each other."*

2. Put students into groups of three or four.

3. Review student directions.

4. Distribute a piece of scrap paper and pen to each group and tell them to identify a recorder for their group.

MODEL AND TEACH

1. Draw students' attention to a list of categories of what they might have in common: dislikes, favorites (foods, colors, places, movies, experiences), future plans, family characteristics (number of siblings, sibling order, etc.).

2. Select a category and model some possible answers, for example, LIKES: "*We all like to eat ice cream. We all like to watch movies. We all like hip-hop.*" **Let the groups know up front that they may not focus on physical attributes.**

PRACTICE AND ASSESS

1. Ask groups to select a recorder and have them discuss for three minutes everything their group members **all** have in common while the recorder takes notes.

2. Circulate, monitor, and support students, as needed. If a group is stuck, ask some questions about one or two of the suggested categories, for example, "*What do you like to do in your free time?*"

3. Use a signal to get the group's attention. Ask the recorders to add up how many things their group has in common.

4. Invite groups to share how many things they have in common by standing up. You might say, "*Stand up if your group has five or more things in common. Ten or more. Fifteen or more. Twenty or more.*"

5. Debrief the class by asking, "*What were some of the most interesting items you discovered you had in common? In what ways might finding out what you have in common help us as a class?*"

Thank students for their active participation.

The next two Activators can be used at the beginning of the year as well as throughout a course to create a High-Performing Community of Learners.

Weather Report

TIME: 5-10 MINUTES

TEACHER PREP LIST

❑ Display student directions

❑ Display types of weather (optional)

STUDENT DIRECTIONS

1. Pick a weather condition that represents _____ .

2. Share your weather condition, and listen attentively to your peers' weather conditions.

SET UP THE ACTIVATOR

1. Explain the purpose of this Activator. You might say, *"This Activator will help us quickly check in on how everyone's first week of school has been. Afterwards, you'll be really ready to focus on today's lesson."* (Alternatively, you could check in on how everyone feels about their group project, writing an essay, math, etc.)

2. Review student directions.

3. Let students know that you will ask them to respond to a check-in question by saying a weather condition that best matches how their first week of school has gone, how they're feeling about their group project, etc.

MODEL AND TEACH

1. To make sure students have a variety of weather conditions to use, brainstorm a list of different types of weather conditions, or post a list of weather conditions for them to refer to.

2. Model for students by going first. Let them know they don't have to explain the reasoning behind their condition unless they really want to.

PRACTICE AND ASSESS

1. Give students 60 seconds of silence to think of their weather condition.

2. Have students share out using the Wave format (Chapter 4).

3. Follow up with a quick statement that normalizes students' responses and acknowledges that everyone is in a different place. This can be a simple way to communicate you care about them as individuals.

4. Before the end of class, check in individually with any students whose weather reports indicate they might benefit from a more personal follow up conversation.

Thank students for their active participation.

VARIATIONS AND EXTENSIONS

Optional: Create a list of weather conditions to project or post for students to refer to. (A complete list of all weather conditions used by the National Weather Service can be found at http://w1.weather.gov/xml/current_obs/weather.php)

Color Chips

Students select and share a color chip that represents their response to a check-in question. In a large class, this Activator works well when done in groups of four or five.

TIME: 5–10 MINUTES

TEACHER PREP LIST

- ❑ Stack of paint color chips from your local hardware store

- ❑ Display color chip options in one of the following ways depending upon the size of your group. For smaller classes (20 students or fewer), spread color chips out on a table and have students gather around. For larger classes you could do one of the following: a) divide the class up into four or five groups and have a set of color chips for each group, b) tape large size color chips around the room and have students choose by going to stand by the color chips, c) use an LCD projector or a SMART board to project a picture of various color chips

- ❑ Display prompt and student directions

STUDENT DIRECTIONS:

1. Select a color chip that represents _____ .

2. Share your color chip and what it represents with the class/your group.

SET UP THE ACTIVATOR

1. Explain the purpose of the Activator. You might say, *"This Activator is called Color Chips and it's a quick and colorful way to check in with everyone. Afterwards you'll be really ready to focus on today's lesson."* Possible prompts: *"What color would you paint our classroom and why? What color represents something from your day? What color gives you energy? (A great prompt for when the collective affect of the class is flat.) What color calms you? (Ask this when a class is acting rowdy and having trouble settling down.) What color reminds you of (insert course title) and why? What color represents how you are feeling about the test tomorrow and why?"*

2. Review student directions.

3. Let students know that you will ask them a check-in question and invite them to pick a color chip that best represents their response. Tell them they will need to briefly explain their choice to the group. (Alternatively, you could have them Turn and Talk with a partner or share out in small groups.)

NOTE: Students often respond as much to the color as the name of the color, so be sure to grab some with interesting names like "Duct Tape," "Jamaica Me Crazy," or "Buttered Popcorn." Also, while most adolescents respond with immediate interest when they spot the color chips, using colors as metaphors requires higher-level thinking and some students might struggle. Consider first asking a more concrete question such as, "*What color would you paint our class and why?*" the first time you introduce color chips.

MODEL AND TEACH

1. Model how you expect students to share out by going first. For example, "*I picked 'Sunshiny Day' because I think it would make this room a fun place to work and think.*" Or "*I picked this light blue color called 'Calm Seas' because it seems like a peaceful color and I have noticed this group has been really respectful to each other.*"

PRACTICE AND ASSESS

1. Give students 60 seconds of think time to pick their own color chip and formulate their response. Let students know it is okay to share a color if someone else chooses the same color chip as they do. Simply have them pass it to the other person when it is their turn to share.

2. If doing this Activator as a whole group, have students share out using the Popcorn format (Chapter 3). If students are sharing with a partner or in a small group, circulate to monitor on-task conversations.

3. Debrief by asking students to share some highlights from their sharing in small groups or by asking what patterns they noticed in the whole group's responses.

Thank students for their active participation.

> *It is only when we understand what our students are thinking, feeling, and attending to that we can use that knowledge to further engage and support them in the process of understanding. Thus making students' thinking visible becomes an ongoing component of effective teaching.*
>
> —Ron Ritchhart, Mark Church and Karin Morrison

Post It Up

Students create a data "visual" that serves as a springboard for a learning-focused dialogue.

We live in a data-obsessed age, and Post It Up is an Activator that provides both the students and the teacher with a data visual to examine, discuss, and learn from. The key component of a Post It Up Activator is that students vote or visibly display a snapshot of their thinking or responses on a whiteboard, wall, piece of poster paper, or table by using sticky notes (Post-it brand or similar), sticker dots/stars, or initials. The power of this Activator comes with the rich dialogue that follows the Post It Up. The data picture that is generated serves to foster curiosity, connections, and deep thinking.

What are the ways the Post It Up Activator supports the conditions for engagement?

- Garners **good will** by welcoming multiple perspectives
- Supports **participation** by creating a platform for everyone's voice while also allowing for anonymity
- Captures **attention** by providing a concrete visual and incorporating movement

- Increases **interest** by creating an opportunity for students to consider how their thinking is similar or different from their peers
- Supports **effort** by emphasizing that everyone's "vote" counts and is an important part of the big picture
- Fosters **investment** by providing a way to gather data around Classroom Expectations and Classroom Agreements

TIME: 5-15 MINUTES

TEACHER PREP LIST

- ❏ Sticker dots, star stickers, sticky notes, or pens/markers and chart paper/ whiteboard

- ❏ If using sticker dots, star stickers, or sticky notes, prepare them for easy distribution. For example, if you have table groups of four, you might put a strip of four pre-cut sticker dots on each table

- ❏ Identify a space for students to place their "votes": whiteboard, wall area, chart paper, or table top

- ❏ Design an engaging prompt aligned with a learning outcome

- ❏ Display prompt and student directions

- ❏ Design debrief questions to support a thoughtful examination and reflection of the data

ACTIVATOR SNAPSHOT

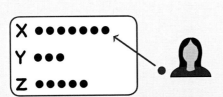

STUDENT DIRECTIONS

1. Consider the Post It Up question and review the optional responses.

2. At the signal, vote for your option(s) by placing a star, dot, etc. in the designated space on the poster.

3. Return to your seat, begin examining the data, and prepare to debrief with the class.

SET UP THE ACTIVATOR

1. Explain the purpose of the Activator. You might say, *"We're going to do an Activator that will quickly create a snapshot of everyone's thinking about _____ , and keep your brains alert by putting you on your feet. We will then step back to discuss what we see in order to deepen our learning."*

2. Review student directions.

3. Display and read the prompt.

MODEL AND TEACH

1. Model how to place a sticker/sticky note or mark a "vote" with a pen or marker. If using stickers/sticky notes, demonstrate how to place these without covering up the words that are displayed. If using pens or markers, model the size students should make their mark.

2. If students need support in deciding "how" to vote, model by using a different prompt and doing a Think Aloud.

PRACTICE AND ASSESS

1. Tell students how much time they have to place their stickers/sticky notes or make their marks and ask them to begin.

2. Remind students when time is halfway up.

3. When the time is up, use a signal to get the group's attention, and debrief the Activator by asking the class some of the following generic questions here or generate your own more specific ones:

Content Questions
- What do you see or notice?
- So what do you think it means or why does it matter?
- Now what should we be asking, doing, or trying to understand?

Process Questions
- How does seeing a visual like this impact your thinking?
- What influenced your decision for how you voted?

Thank students for their active participation, affirm understandings, and address any misconceptions that surfaced.

TROUBLESHOOTING TIPS

- Sticky notes and sticker dots create a nice visual and students react positively to the tactile task, but these items do cost money so consider having students draw a star or a make a tally mark on chart paper or the whiteboard when supply costs are an issue.
- To maximize participation in the debrief, use a strategy like Quick Jot▪, Quick Draw▪, Table Talk▪, Cold Calls▪, Numbered Heads▪, or Turn and Talk (Chapter 3).

- If you have space constraints in your room, you may need to stagger the time for the Post It Up process, or have two different posters and designate one half of the room for each, and then bring both posters to the front for the debrief.

VARIATIONS AND EXTENSIONS

- Have students work in table groups to generate a smaller set of data that they can then manipulate by organizing the sticky notes into categories. Afterwards, table groups can do a gallery walk to see and reflect on the way other groups organized their sticky notes. (See the biology example on page 61.)
- Give students two or more different colored dots to indicate different "votes" on the same poster. (See the ELA Speaking/Listening example on page 63).

Using Post It Up to Create a High-Performing Community of Learners

6

In our visits to classrooms around the country we frequently see Post It Up used at the beginning of a year, semester, or trimester as a forum for individual student goal setting, and often those goals remain posted in the room. Teachers and students refer to the goals frequently to support Habits of Learning, like practicing the critical skill of -monitoring their own learning and progress in each of their subject areas. A Post It Up Activator that requires students to reflect on their own competency with the identified unit standards or objectives is one way to keep the class focused on the prioritized outcomes. And by its very nature, this Activator fosters a sense of connectedness because of the way it collects and projects a snapshot of the group's collective thoughts and opinions.

Research shows that collaborative learning is a powerful tool for student achievement (Johnson & Johnson, 1988), yet most students need support to be able to collaborate effectively with their peers. Having a small group do a Post It Up Activator where they identify essential group behaviors and discuss what they need from each other will support them to function effectively and efficiently on their group task. This type of data helps students to harness their empathy and understanding for others and helps them see their peers as individuals with similar or different needs when working independently and within the group. Using Post It Up provides students with real-time data to inform what steps they need to take to strengthen their relationships for the important work they need to do with each other.

Post It Up Examples for Creating a High-Performing Community of Learners

- Mark your initials by the unit standard that is most challenging for you.
- Put a star sticker by the college and career readiness standards you feel will be most important for your personal college and career aspirations.

- (In project groups) Review the list of essential collaboration norms and select the one you feel is most important for your group to pay attention to over the course of the project. Each group member should write down their own norm on a sticky note and place it in the center of your group's table. Then each group should examine all the sticky notes and follow the generic debrief protocol: **What?** *"What did group members pick?"* **So What?** *"Why are these important?"* And **Now What?** *"What can we do as individuals and a group to make sure we are paying attention to and upholding these norms?"*

- On a sticky note, set a specific goal for improving in one of the four Habits of Learning categories and sign your name to it. Post your note on the Goal Setting for Next Unit poster in the back of the room, placing it in the quadrant that coincides with the Habit of Learning you selected (see example below).

Prompt and In Class	**Organized and Prepared**
On-task and Engaged	**High-Quality Work**

Using Post It Up to Support Learning in the Content Areas

Generate Connections to Prior Knowledge: Using Post It Up to solicit and record predictions or assumptions about a topic is a natural fit for this Activator. For example, in a world language class that is structured thematically, Post It Up can be used to help students anticipate the vocabulary they will need to learn in the next unit on holidays and celebrations. When the new unit vocabulary is presented, students can examine how accurate they were at predicting the vocabulary. This simple Post It Up can easily lead to a deeper discussion on how culture influences language; students might not have thought of a high-frequency word because it is not part of or as important in their own culture.

Provide Opportunities to Practice Skills and Deepen Understanding: Post It Up Activators are particularly impactful because they create a visual that serves as a permanent anchor for student understanding. When economics students use the Post It Up Activator to generate a real-life example of how supply and demand influences prices, they create a visual that makes this essential economic concept come to life. And when students hear about a political candidate being on the "far left" or the "far right" they can access a mental image of the political spectrum where they were asked to plot their own political beliefs and also know that political stances are much more complex than simply "left" or "right."

Support Formative Assessment: Post It Up can be used to measure student understanding and clarify where there might be confusion. When a teacher has students place a sticker dot next to the unit concepts they find most confusing and draw a star next to the unit concept they are feeling confident about, that teacher gains immediate insight about where to focus re-teaching efforts. It can also be a way to create or identify small groups with similar academic needs to allow the teacher to differentiate instruction.

Inject Relevance Into the Curriculum: Post It Up Activators can also be used to tie your content to world issues or student interests. For example, you could list career areas that are related to your subject and have students do a Post It Up to indicate which they are most interested in. By connecting your content to students' career interest you open the door for making your class relevant to their futures and personal interests.

6

Math

Algebra

Place a dot on the method would you use to solve for this system of equations.

$$y = -3x - 7$$
$$-5x + y = 1$$

1. Graph them and find the point of intersection
2. Make tables for both and look for the point of intersection
3. Solve it algebraically using substitution
4. Solve it algebraically using elimination

Write out your solution on a sticky note and post it next to the letter that corresponds with your response. Be prepared to explain why your method is best.

Geometry

Review the standards that were included in this unit. Place a star sticker next to the standards that you would like to focus on during the review day.

1. Understand similarity in terms of similarity transformations
2. Prove theorems involving similarity
3. Define trigonometric ratios and solve problems involving right triangles
4. Apply geometric concepts in modeling situations
5. Apply trigonometry to general triangles

Science

Earth Science

Examine the different career options related to earth science. Put your initials by the one you would be most interested in. Be prepared to facilitate a discussion around the way the careers might relate to earth science.

- Lawyer
- Graphic Designer
- Engineer
- Writer
- Computer Programmer

- Chemist
- Forest Ranger
- Politician
- Meteorologist
- Oceanographer
- Fire Fighter
- Teacher

Biology

In table groups, on sticky notes, jot down five to seven individual food items you've eaten today. Afterwards, move the sticky notes around on your table to sort them into organic compound categories:

- Carbohydrates
- Proteins
- Nucleic acids
- Lipids

Chemistry

Place your dot sticker (or draw an X) on the continuum that represents your response to the following question:

"We will be doing labs once a week in this course. How do you feel about doing lab activities and handling chemicals?"

Very confident and comfortable _____Not at all confident and comfortable

Physics

Put a green dot sticker next to a concept you feel confident explaining to a neighbor and a red dot next to a concept you need further support in understanding.

- Circular motion
- Rotational inertia
- Torque
- Centripetal force
- Centrifugal force

Social Studies

Economics

Supply and Demand graph – Place your dot sticker on the graph to show how much you would be willing to pay for one slice of chocolate cake right now. Next let students know that there are only 10 slices of cake and ask them to determine what each cake slice would probably cost, given their data.

U.S. History

Place your dot sticker on the continuum to indicate how skillfully you feel President Kennedy handled the Cuban Missile Crisis.

Very Skillful _____ Not Very Skillful

World History

Place a star sticker on the continuum to represent your response to the following statement:

The consequences of China's industrialization and economic growth are:

Mostly Positive _____ Mostly Negative

Government

Initial Post It Up:

Place a star sticker on the political compass chart to indicate where you think you might fall.

Follow-up Post It Up

After students take a political spectrum quiz and you have explained the political compass chart: place your dot sticker on the chart based on your political spectrum quiz result.

(Search the internet to find a printable political compass charts and political spectrum quizzes.)

English Language Arts

Writing

Write your initials next to an aspect of your persuasive speech you are feeling good about and an exclamation point "!" next to an aspect of your persuasive speech you are feeling challenged by:

- Introducing precise claims
- Establishing the significance of claims
- Distinguishing claims from counterclaims
- Supplying evidence for claims and counterclaims
- Pointing out strengths and limitations of claims and counterclaims

Reading – Literature

Put a sticky note next to the sign that represents your response to the following statement:

The conflict in the novel *47* is unresolved at the end.

True / True with Modifications / Not True / Unable to determine

Reading – Informational Texts

Put a star or dot sticker next to the component that would be most helpful to you in reading a chapter in your textbook:

- Headings and subheadings
- Italicized words
- Summary at the end of the chapter
- Review questions at the end of the chapter
- Charts and graphs
- Pictures and captions

Speaking and Listening

Put a green dot sticker by one thing you did really well during today's conversation and put a blue dot by one thing you want to be more intentional in practicing next time:

- Using textual evidence to support ideas
- Posing questions that connect our discussion to larger ideas
- Actively engaging others in the conversation
- Clarifying each other's ideas and conclusions
- Verifying each other's ideas
- Challenging each other's ideas respectfully

Language

Draw an X along the strongly agree-strongly disagree continuum in a position that represents your response to the following statement:

" I can distinguish between when I need to use a semi-colon (;) and when I need to use a colon (:) in a sentence."

World Languages

On the 3x5 size sticky notes, using a black marker, write down two to three vocabulary words (in English) that you think will be important to learn and know during our next unit on _____ . Be sure you write them large and clear enough for students at the back of the room to read when we post these on the whiteboard.

Put your initials by the aspect of learning a language that you find most challenging:

- Vocabulary
- Grammar
- Speaking and pronunciation
- Reading
- Listening

Put a dot sticker next to the career area in (the target language) you are most interested in.

Suggestions for Writing Your Own Post It Up Activators:

Consider integrating at least two quick and low-prep Post It Up Activators into your unit. You might include one at the beginning of the unit to allow students to voice their opinion on a concept, and a second one at the end of the unit to solicit feedback on which concepts, skills, and knowledge students are struggling with.

YOUR TURN

Design Your Own Post It Up Activators

A Checklist for Designing Effective Activators:

☐ *Does the prompt support a specific learning outcome?*

☐ *Is the prompt engaging?* Can students respond without feeling anxious or uncomfortable? Do students have enough prior knowledge to feel competent in their responses? Will the prompt ignite curiosity, make content relevant, and challenge students to think at a high level?

☐ *Is the prompt crafted with invitational language that promotes exploration and reduces the need for certainty?* Invitational prompts might begin with "What might...?" "What are some of the...?" or "What is your hunch for why...?"

6

7

We focus on the outside world in education and don't look much at inwardly focused reflective skills and attentions, but inward focus impacts the way we build memories, make meaning and transfer that learning into new contexts... What are we doing in schools to support kids turning inward?

—MARY HELEN IMMORDINO-YANG

Silent Conversation

Students engage in a silent content-based "conversation" by exchanging written notes back and forth with a partner.

Any student who has ever passed a note in class (or texted) enjoys Silent Conversation. This Activator creates curiosity and anticipation (*"How will my partner respond? What's everybody else writing about?"*), and capitalizes on adolescents' need to express themselves. The hush that descends upon the room during Silent Conversation changes up the classroom dynamic and is a boon for more introverted students who need and appreciate the quiet reflection it affords. Exchanging papers back and forth coupled with sitting in silence slows all students down long enough to hear their own voices, discover new ideas, engage in deep thinking, and pay respectful attention to their partners' perspectives.

What are the ways the Silent Conversation Activator supports the conditions for engagement?

- Garners **good will** by valuing what students have to say
- Supports **participation** by creating connectedness through partnering with another student
- Captures **attention** by providing an audience for students' writing

- Increases **interest** by injecting novelty and relevance
- Fosters **effort** by encouraging students to explore their thinking
- Supports **investment** when serving as vehicle to reflect on Classroom Expectations and Classroom Agreements

TIME: 5-10 MINUTES

TEACHER PREP LIST

- ❑ Design an engaging prompt aligned with a learning outcome that invites divergent perspectives
- ❑ Display prompt and student directions
- ❑ Determine how you will pair students
- ❑ Timer

ACTIVATOR SNAPSHOT

STUDENT DIRECTIONS

1. Each pair needs one piece of paper and two writing utensils.

2. Decide which partner will begin the conversation.

3. After some individual think time, jot down a response to the prompt and pass the paper to your partner.

4. Respond by answering and asking questions, providing details and making connections, and return the paper to your partner. Continue until the time is up.

SET UP THE ACTIVATOR

1. Explain the purpose of the Activator. You might say, *"We're going to do an Activator called Silent Conversation. The purpose is to give you time to explore your ideas about _____ by exchanging notes with a partner. Because the conversation is silent and happens on paper, you get to think deeply and really pay attention to what your partner has to say. I realize it might feel strange to sit in silence while your partner is writing, and I'm going to ask you to give it a try. I'm confident it will help everyone slow down long enough to do some really smart thinking."*

2. Review student directions. Explain that one of the students will begin by writing a brief response on the paper and then hand the paper over to the partner to respond.

3. Pair students. If there are an uneven number of students, you can form a trio (ask them to use two different pieces of paper to avoid too much downtime when only one person is writing).

4. Ask students to take out one piece of paper and two writing utensils.

MODEL AND TEACH

1. Ask for a volunteer who is willing to model the beginning of a silent conversation with you in front of the class on the SMART Board, chart paper, or blackboard. Use a different prompt than what the students will respond to, and model ways of moving the conversation along with your partner by asking questions, making connections, and supporting opinions with evidence.

2. Ask students to share what they noticed about how you kept the conversation going.

3. Show an additional model of a brief Silent Conversation (either projected or typed up) and ask students what they notice each partner does that keeps the conversation moving. (We have provided a Sample Silent Conversation for this purpose.)

4. Tell students they will have three to four minutes for their Silent Conversation. Ask students to be mindful of any relevant Classroom Expectations or Classroom Agreements which would apply to silent, written communication as well. If you will be collecting students' papers afterwards, let them know. Emphasize that students should avoid editing each other's writing; the focus of this Activator is on what students think and write, not on whether they spell or use punctuation correctly.

Sample Silent Conversation

If you were a teacher, what are some ways you would keep students your age interested in learning?

A: "Hmmm, let's see. I know I really like it when my social studies teacher tells interesting stories about real people from history. That's so much better than reading stuff from the textbook. What do you think?"

B: "Stories are always fun. I used to have a math teacher who would make up word problem stories using kids' names from our class. That was cool."

A: "I love math, because it's like a puzzle you have to solve. It's even more fun when we get to move things around to figure out a problem, like toothpicks or cubes or something."

B: "That would be fun; I never did that. I like it when I get to work with other students in math to figure out a problem. Really, I like any class where we get to work in groups. What about you?"

A: "I usually like working on my own, although we just did a debate about social media in English and that was pretty interesting."

B: "Debates make anything more fun, but it's definitely easier when you get to pick the side you want to be on."

PRACTICE AND ASSESS

1. Set a timer and begin. Circulate, monitor, and support students' active participation and learning.

2. Offer some feedback that affirms efforts and reminds students of expectations. For example, "*I notice you're elaborating on your responses. Remember to ask your partners to explain their thinking.*"

3. Periodically remind students of time remaining.

4. Use a signal to get the group's attention and begin the debrief using some of the following content and process questions:

Content Questions
- What is something your partner wrote about _____ that stood out to you?
- What did you realize about _____ ?
- What are you wondering about _____ ?

Process Questions
- What was it like to engage in a silent conversation?
- What are the ways this was similar and different to oral communication?
- What connections can you make between how you "talked" to your partner in this Activator and our Classroom Expectations and Classroom Agreements?

Thank students for their active participation, affirm understandings, and address any misconceptions that surfaced.

TROUBLESHOOTING TIPS

- Carry a pad of sticky notes as you circulate around the room. If a student gets stuck and doesn't know what to write, scan the conversation and jot down a quick note that might move the student in the right direction and leave it on the desk.

- If you notice some students are challenged in sustaining a conversation, conduct a follow-up mini-lesson using student exemplars to unpack successful Silent Conversation moves.

- Front-load a reminder that Group Agreements apply to all forms of communication, and emphasize a focus on content as opposed to correct grammar and spelling.

- If students struggle to stay quiet, start with a very short Silent Conversation and work up to longer ones.

- Play music during Silent Conversation, which can increase students' comfort with the silence required during this Activator.

VARIATIONS AND EXTENSIONS

- Provide students with two different colored pens in order to highlight the two writers' ideas.

- Have students use classroom or mini whiteboards instead of paper.

- Give each partner his/her own piece of paper or whiteboard; students simultaneously write and respond to each other using the same or two different prompts. Ask them to put a "/" to indicate when they switch turns.

- Invite a few pairs to share some of their Silent Conversation aloud with the class.

- Ask students to highlight a piece of their Silent Conversation that gets at the heart of what they discussed. "Publish" some of these back to the class the next day for reflection and discussion.

- Ask students to review their conversations to find claims, supporting evidence, and counterclaims.

- Collect the Silent Conversation papers, jot down responses, and make copies for each partner that they can use in preparation for unit assessments.

- Put students into groups of four and ask everyone to write a response to either the same prompt or different prompts on four individual pieces of paper. When students are done responding, invite them to pass their papers to the person on their right who should write down a comment before passing it on to the next person. Continue until the writer gets her paper back with responses from all the group members.

Using Silent Conversation to Create a High-Performing Community of Learners

Silent Conversation fosters Trust and a Belonging by providing opportunities for one-to-one connections that can add up to a High-Performing Community of Learners. As students share with one other classmate their hopes for what they might learn before graduating high school, they find out things they may not have known about each other. This can increase their comfort working together as newly assigned partners on a project and also provides important information the teacher can use to connect to individual students and meet their needs and interests as the year unfolds. The Trust and Belonging that grow between partners as well as among students and the teacher drive the class towards its target of being a High-Performing Community of Learners.

The inherent nature of this Activator format encourages behaviors that create a High-Performing Community of Learners. A Silent Conversation Activator asks students to: take turns, acknowledge and welcome alternate perspectives, allow one person to speak at a time, share the talk space, and listen. As a result, it is a great vehicle for kick-starting students' thinking in anticipation of crafting Classroom Agreements. Ideas generated about "community" during Silent Conversation can be used to design Classroom Agreements that will help a class be a safe and productive space for everyone, especially around topics that might be sensitive like immigration policies, cultural differences, genetic testing or evolution.

7

Silent Conversation Examples for Creating a High-Performing Community of Learners

- What are some things you think of when you hear the word "community?"
- What are some things you would like to learn before you graduate from high school?
- If you were a teacher, what are some ways you would keep students your age interested in learning?

Using Silent Conversation to Support Learning in the Content Areas

Generate Connections to Prior Knowledge: Silent Conversation can bring a laser focus to the beginning of a unit or new topic. Asking students to engage in a Silent Conversation around what it means to be American at the beginning of a unit that explores this question helps them activate prior knowledge while creating an artifact of their thinking. At the end of the unit, students can revisit these conversations to reflect on new understandings and deepen their learning.

Provide Opportunities to Practice Skills and Deepen Understanding: Students can use this Activator to slow down and process content with a partner. After watching a video and reading a text on the Crusades, a world history class teacher might direct students to use Silent Conversation to ask and respond to questions they have about the Crusades. To help students get started, the teacher might provide a compelling question as a model, for example, *"Given that the Crusades lasted 177 years, what impact might they have on how people in the Middle East currently view Westerners?"* Encouraging students to self-generate and silently "discuss" questions helps them make sense of what they've taken in from multiple sources. It is also a safe way of asking questions that adolescents might not be comfortable raising with the larger group.

Conduct Formative Assessment: Silent Conversation is effective for providing immediate feedback to students learning a new skill or concept. While algebra students solve for "x" together, they make their thinking transparent to peers who can question, clarify, challenge or confirm their ideas. Observing students during this process, the teacher quickly sees who is actively working out solutions as well as who might be struggling. And by asking students to document their Silent Conversation on paper and collecting them, the teacher can get a closer look at where students are on track as well as how to follow up later in the lesson or the next day by addressing any gaps in understanding.

Review Prior to an Assessment: This Activator offers a way to actively study while also having a little fun. World language students who craft a Silent Conversation with a "pen pal" in the target language around birthday celebrations are practicing how to use key unit vocabulary and grammar. This active rehearsal leads to storing information in long-term memory that will come in handy on the unit test.

Make Connections Beyond the Content: The opportunity to have an extended conversation on paper with a peer makes this Activator a natural for connecting the classroom to larger societal issues. After reading an article about the Henrietta Lacks case (Skloot, 2000) in a biology unit on the nature of cancerous cells, Silent Conversation might be used to explore the ethical issues involved in harvesting Henrietta's cells for medical research without her consent. By making a unit on cancerous cells more complex in this way, a biology teacher draws real-life connections that can hook otherwise unmotivated students and inspire others to discover a passion.

Math

Algebra

Solve for x, show all steps:

$4x + 7 = 10 + x$

$x^2 + 7x + 12 = 0$

$x^2 - x - 20 = 0$

$x^2 - 7x = -10$

Geometry

What is the length of the side labeled m? Show all work.

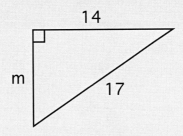

Science

Earth Science

What are some ways renewable resources might be good for the environment?

Biology

To what extent was it ethical for Henrietta Lacks' doctors to harvest her cells without explicitly telling her their intentions? What are some reasons to support your argument?

Chemistry

Should we use nuclear energy? What are some reasons to support your argument?

Physics

What are some ways you can determine your average speed of walking?

Social Studies

Geography

After reading about the culture of teen girls and boys in Saudi Arabia (or another country), write notes to your partner about the cultural aspects you found most interesting or surprising and identify similarities and differences between your culture and the culture described in the reading.

U.S. History

Pick a role and engage in a Silent Conversation where you share your thoughts on the Vietnam War from your perspective. Possible roles: U.S. soldier, protester, parent of soldier, Vietnamese villager, Viet Cong, President Johnson, President Nixon, Ho Chi Minh.

World History

Using the video clip and the text as a source, write and respond to questions you have about the Crusades. Be prepared to share specific content questions as well as deeper thinking or larger concept questions with the rest of the class.

Government

What are some characteristics of a "good" government? What are some characteristics of a "bad" government? Be sure to include and discuss specific examples.

English Language Arts

Writing

Prior to writing a literary essay, create a dialogue of authors: George Orwell and William Golding discussing what *Lord of The Flies* and *Shooting an Elephant* reveal about human nature (each student writes from the point of view of one of the authors).

Reading - Literature

What might be "wrong" with Holden? What are some pieces of evidence you might use to support your claim? (During a unit on *Catcher in the Rye*.)

Reading - Informational Texts

What does it mean to be American?

Language

Use seven of our unit's vocabulary words accurately in a Silent Conversation using your own scenario or one of the following:

1.) Teen trying to convince parent to let them date someone parent doesn't want them to.

2.) Aliens from two different planets debating about which planet is a better place to live.

3.) Two friends debating which movie they will go to this weekend.

4.) A cat and a dog debating about who is the better pet.

World Languages

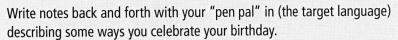

Write notes back and forth with your "pen pal" in (the target language) describing some ways you celebrate your birthday.

Write notes back and forth with your "pen pal" in (the target language) describing a shopping trip you went on and what you purchased.

Write notes back and forth with your partner in (the target language) asking them about what sports they like to play/watch.

7

Suggestions for Writing Your Own Silent Conversation Activators

Scan your unit to look for key understandings, knowledge, or skills that lend themselves to dialogue or debate. This Activator is also great to use when you want to have concrete examples of what students are thinking and understanding for formative assessment purposes. What questions or problems might you pose that students would benefit from exploring in this way?

YOUR TURN

Design Your Own Silent Conversation Activators

A Checklist for Designing Effective Activators:

- ☐ *Does the prompt support a specific learning outcome?*

- ☐ *Is the prompt engaging?* Can students respond without feeling anxious or uncomfortable? Do students have enough prior knowledge to feel competent in their responses? Will the prompt ignite curiosity, make content relevant, and challenge students to think at a high level?

- ☐ *Is the prompt crafted with invitational language that promotes exploration and reduces the need for certainty?* Invitational prompts might begin with "What might...?" "What are some of the...?" or "What is your hunch for why...?"

*In a brain compatible classroom, assessment both
measures achievement and provides motivation.*

—D. Judy Stevens and Dee Goldberg

Mini Whiteboard

Students work collaboratively to respond to prompts
by writing on individual-sized whiteboards.

Mini whiteboards are showing up in classrooms across the country because their impact on student engagement is instantaneous. We have yet to find a student who does not love to write on whiteboards, erase the whiteboard, and then immediately want to do it all over again. While some teachers have students use whiteboards only for individual student practice, mini whiteboards are a perfect tool for having students think and work collaboratively in the form of an Activator. The Mini Whiteboard Activator serves to engage pairs or small groups in creating a product to hold up, making their thinking visible for the rest of the class so that they can self-check their understanding on knowledge or skills. When used for more open-ended prompts, it serves to expose the whole class to a variety of ideas, examples, and creative thinking.

Materials Tip: While you can order sets of whiteboards easily over the Internet for a little less than two dollars a board, there is a much more cost effective way of outfitting your classroom with a set of personal-sized whiteboards. Big chain home improvement stores carry pieces of white glossy shower board. Find a friendly employee and ask him/her to cut it up into squares measuring roughly 12x12 inches (cutting lumber for customers is part of their service). At the writing of this book, a single sheet of shower board costs between 11 and 14 dollars and can be cut up into 30 individual-size boards. Instead of erasers, use socks that have lost their mates, cut up a few old t-shirts, or spend a few dollars on a half-yard of felt at a craft or fabric store and cut it up into small eraser-size squares. Dry erase markers are the most costly aspect of using mini whiteboards, so it pays to watch for sales. We recommend storing sets of them in zip-top bags. We find that teachers feel that their small investment is well worth it.

What are the ways the Mini Whiteboard Activator supports the conditions for engagement?

- Garners **good will** by integrating materials that make learning interactive
- Supports **participation** by offering a task that is both fun and low-risk
- Captures **attention** by providing tactile, hands-on materials
- Increases **interest** by creating an opportunity for students to collaborate, compete, or be creative
- Supports **effort** by creating an opportunity for everyone to actively practice skills and knowledge, and get immediate feedback
- Fosters **investment** by providing a way to share thinking around Classroom Expectations and Classroom Agreements

TIME: 10-15 MINUTES

TEACHER PREP LIST

- ❑ Whiteboards for each pair/trio
- ❑ Dry erase markers for each pair/trio
- ❑ Erasers for each pair or trio (socks, felt squares, and cut up old t-shirts work fine)
- ❑ Timer
- ❑ Determine your strategy for distributing materials. You might have small stacks of whiteboards at each table, or appoint students to be Materials Managers and have them distribute the boards, markers, and erasers in a systematic way
- ❑ Design an engaging prompt aligned with a learning outcome that does not require a lengthy response
- ❑ Determine how you will group students
- ❑ Display prompt and student directions and sentence starters, if using
- ❑ Prepare a sample Mini Whiteboard response to show as a model

ACTIVATOR SNAPSHOT

STUDENT DIRECTIONS

1. Think about your response to the prompt.

2. Discuss your responses to the prompt with your partner(s).

3. Decide how you will share writing your response on the mini whiteboard.

4. Collaborate to develop a group response and write this on the mini whiteboard.

SET UP THE ACTIVATOR

1. Explain the purpose of the Activator. You might say, *"Today we are going to use mini whiteboards because they are a fun way for everyone to actively practice the skills/knowledge we have been learning. Using mini whiteboards in pairs or trios requires you to show what you know and you get to find out right away if you are on the right track."* A more open-ended prompt would sound like, *"Today I am going to push you to think deeply and creatively using the mini whiteboards, and when you hold them up we will all benefit from seeing the wide range of responses from your classmates."*

2. Review student directions.

3. Because students can get distracted once they get their hands on a mini whiteboard and dry erase marker, it is important to give clear directions in advance of giving them access to the markers. Say, *"Keep your zip-top bag of dry erase markers and eraser squares closed until I say go."*

4. Group students into pairs or trios and distribute a mini whiteboard, dry erase markers, and an "eraser" to each group.

MODEL AND TEACH

1. Show a model Mini Whiteboard response that demonstrates your expectations about print/image size, as well as neatness to ensure students can read each other's boards when they hold them up. Ask students what they notice.

2. Emphasize your expectation that students will collaborate and discuss what they are going to write/draw in response to the prompt prior to launching in. You might offer some sentence starters for this purpose, for example, *"Does everyone think we should write _____?"* or *"What does everyone think about _____?"* or *"It sounds like we're saying _____."*

3. Remind students of any relevant Classroom Expectations and Classroom Agreements and articulate the expectation that students focus on the content of others' responses rather than the spelling or grammar.

PRACTICE AND ASSESS

1. Let students know exactly how many minutes they have to complete the task. Announce the start time, set your timer, and have students begin.

2. Circulate, monitor, and support students' active participation and learning.

3. When time is up, ask pairs or small groups to hold up their whiteboards. Note: Consider why you are having students hold up their whiteboard for your particular Activator and adjust your instructions accordingly. Is it simply a way to hold all students accountable for being on task? Is it for you to see if they arrived at a correct answer? If so, students don't need to see everyone else's board and this can be a relatively quick process. On the other hand, is your intent that all students will see a variety of perspectives and thinking? If that's the case, consider having them write only a few words and slowly rotate the boards so they are visible to all.

4. Use a signal to get the group's attention, and call on a few pairs/trios to share out what they wrote or describe their drawing. If you're asking a series of questions, instruct students to wipe their boards clean and continue with the next prompt or task.

5. Debrief by asking some of the following content and process questions:

Content questions
- What are some trends you noticed in some of the responses?
- What are some things you learned from the groups' mini whiteboards?
- Are there any responses you have questions about?

Process questions
- What strategies did you use to come up with your response?
- Did anyone approach the prompt/task in a unique way?
- How has this activity helped you learn the information?
- If you could do it again, what would you change or do differently?

Thank students for their active participation, affirm understandings, and address any misconceptions that surfaced.

NOTE: When you're done, provide clear instructions for cleaning up. You might say, "*I need everyone to return the four markers—making sure the caps are on tight—and the four eraser squares to the zip-top bag at their table and zip the bag closed. Stack the boards and the bags up neatly on the corner of your table. These supplies are expensive, so I appreciate your taking good care of them.*"

TROUBLESHOOTING TIPS

- If pairs or trios argue about who gets to write on the whiteboard, assign each partner a portion of the task.

- If participation in the groups is uneven, ask everyone to do a Quick Jot or Quick Draw in their notebook first—before they talk with their group—about what goes on the Mini Whiteboard. This can strengthen accountability.

VARIATIONS AND EXTENSIONS

- If you want students to linger longer over the response and really analyze what other students have written on their boards, consider an alternative to the hold-up aspect of the Activator. Instead you might have them showcase their boards on the chalkboard/whiteboard tray in your room, have them pass their whiteboards around to other groups, or have students place their whiteboards in a line on the floor so everyone can do a silent gallery walk to examine what their classmates have written or drawn.

- Drawing engages both sides of the brain, so take advantage of the Mini Whiteboard's potential by having students respond to questions and prompts in a variety of ways including drawing symbols, pictures, or diagrams.

8

Using Mini Whiteboard to Create a High-Performing Community of Learners

Because adolescents react so positively to whiteboards, the Mini Whiteboard Activator is a great way to get students to self-reflect and talk about what they need from you and from each other to feel comfortable and be successful learners. Asking students to reflect on and name the characteristics of an ideal class via the whiteboards makes it easy for them to dialogue about a topic that many adolescents might otherwise be hesitant to talk about. When students identify the characteristic of an ideal class, a teacher then has the opportunity to invite students to recreate those same conditions. This metacognitive process helps students to understand that they can and do have the ability to create the classroom culture they want.

Mini Whiteboard can also be used to help students become self-aware of their own learning styles. Asking students to draw a symbol as a way to share with you (and each other) how they learn best communicates that you understand and value individual learning styles. When they hold up their whiteboards, you also have valuable information about the students in your room. By having each student share a whiteboard with a partner, giving each partner a chance to draw their own symbol, and then seeing all the other students' symbols normalizes that everyone has different learning strengths. And because Mini Whiteboard also appeals to learners who need visuals and tactile experiences to learn best, you are building trust with the group by showing that you will intentionally infuse your class with activities to support the variety of ways students learn.

Mini Whiteboard Examples for Creating a High-Performing Community of Learners

- Think of a class that you really enjoyed and where you learned a lot. Make a list of some of the things that made you enjoy that class and the things that helped you be so successful as a learner.
- Draw a symbol to represent the way you learn best.

Using Mini Whiteboard to Support Learning in the Content Areas

Generate Connections to Prior Knowledge: Whiteboards are easily used to brainstorm ideas on a particular topic or help students make connections to their background knowledge. When a world language teacher asks students to write down three adjectives (in the target language) that can be used to describe a person's appearance, every student has an engaging way to reflect on what they know and have the benefit of seeing their classmates' background knowledge as well. What makes Mini Whiteboards even more flexible is the ability to extend making connections beyond words by using symbols and drawings.

Provide Opportunities to Practice Skills and Deepen Understanding: When students are learning a new skill, the Mini Whiteboard Activator provides a great forum for practice. When a social studies teacher has students identify the symbols in a political cartoon and infer their meaning, it supports students as they practice the steps necessary to accurately analyze a political cartoon. Following this up by having students write what they understand the cartoon's message to be, pushes students to think deeply about the cartoon's content and connect it to what they are learning about the topic they are studying.

Prepare Students for an Assessment: The Mini Whiteboard Activator is great for preparing students for an assessment while formatively assessing individual student understanding. For example, in math class you can project or write problems on the board and have students work in pairs to solve them. Once they are ready, have students raise their whiteboards in the air or rest them on their tables facing you. You can glance around the room and see every student's answer very quickly. In this example it is not necessary to direct students to look at everyone else's responses, as you are simply looking for common mistakes. Mistakes are a gem in math classrooms, and Mini Whiteboard Activators can help you uncover them so that students can ask questions, make conjectures, and understand their own misconceptions prior to taking a summative assessment.

Support Formative Assessment: One of the reasons whiteboards have become so popular is that they are a great tool for checking student understanding. When student thinking is made visible through the whiteboard, it is almost like having a window into students' minds. When used to check for basic understanding of knowledge or skills, trends and outliers stand out immediately as you glance around the room. Asking students to draw a picture to illustrate cell division or annotate the parts and function of a brain provide clear evidence of what students know and don't know. The teacher can then provide immediate feedback, which research shows is critical for students to learn skills and knowledge accurately and efficiently.

Inject Relevance Into the Curriculum: Asking students in a chemistry class to jot down ways that understanding chemistry has helped them in their real life is one example of a straightforward Mini Whiteboard Activator that can connect your classroom content with the real world. When pairs and trios hold up their responses, it is like they are holding up billboards announcing the relevance of your curriculum to their lives outside of school.

8

Math

Algebra

1.) Write an equation for each of these lines:

a.)

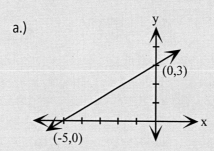

b.)

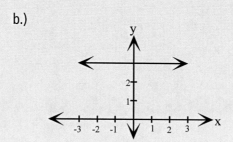

c.)

2.) Solve each of the following equations and show all work.

    a.) $x^2 + x - 20 = 0$

    b.) $3x^2 + 7x = -2$

3.) Solve each of the following equations.

    a.) $|2x + 3| = 4$

    b.) $3(2x - 7) > 10x + 5$

    c.) $|2x - 3| = 13$

Geometry

1.) Solve each of the following equations for r.

    a.) $C = 2\pi r$

    b.) $A = \pi r2$

2.) Jamie has a 2' x 4' pen for her guinea pigs but the mom is pregnant and she needs more space. She wants to make the pen six times as big as it is now.

    a.)   What should the dimensions of the new pen be?

    b.)   Compare the perimeters of the two pens. How much more fencing will she need to buy?

3.) Find the area of the shaded region.

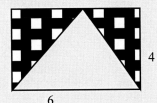

4.) Find the volume and surface area of the following figures.

8

a.)

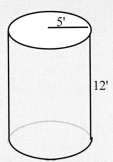

b.)

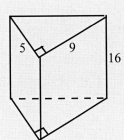

c.)

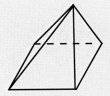

Square base, all edges of the pyramid have length of 8 inches and height of 5.66 inches.

Science

Earth Science
Give an example of how a change in one earth system affects other systems (geosphere, hydrosphere, atmosphere, biosphere)

Biology
Use drawing to explain the cellular process of:
1.) cell division
2.) cell enlargement
3.) cell differentiation

Chemistry
What are three ways chemistry has helped or will help you in your real life?

Physics
Draw a sketch that demonstrates your understanding of probability.

Social Studies

U.S. History
1.) Examine the political cartoon and list three of the symbols used by the artist and explain what they represent. (Example: Uncle Sam = United States government)
2.) Examine the political cartoon and write a statement communicating the artist's message.

World History
1.) List four of the ways the Cold War was fought.
2.) Write a newspaper headline highlighting a key event from the Cold War.

Government
Draw lines to divide your board into four parts:

In the top left corner draw a symbol to represent the concept of Democracy. In the top right corner, draw a symbol to represent the concept of Totalitarianism. In the bottom left corner, draw a symbol to represent the concept of a Republic. In the bottom right corner draw a symbol to represent the concept of a Theocracy.

Psychology

Draw and label the following parts of the brain and list some of the functions under each part:

1.) Cerebrum
2.) Cerebellum
3.) Limbic System
4.) Brain Stem

Follow-up whiteboard hold-up quiz. Which part of the brain:

1.) Receives sensory information? (Limbic system)
2.) Is the largest part of the human brain, associated with higher brain function such as thought and action? (Cerebrum)
3.) Is responsible for basic vital life functions such as breathing, heartbeat, and blood pressure? (Brain stem)
4.) Is associated with regulation and coordination of movement, posture, and balance? (Cerebellum)

English Language Arts

Writing

What are some search term words you might you use to identify the book requested in this posting from a social network site?

Someone needs to help me find this book. It contained Native Americans as the primary protagonists; included witchcraft, gunrunning, and I believe a supporting cast of hippies. Big myth subtext.

Reading – Literature

Create an alternate title for Chapter _____ in _____ .

Reading – Informational Texts

What are three or four words from Lincoln's Second Inaugural Address that seem important, surprising or symbolic to you?

Speaking and Listening

1.) What is one point of agreement you heard in our discussion of the Internet's impact on gender stereotypes?
2.) What is one point of disagreement you heard in our discussion of the Internet's impact on gender stereotypes?

Language

Draw a sketch that represents the meaning of the word _____ .

World Languages

Write down three adjectives you know in (the target language) that can be used to describe a person's appearance. Write down one adjective in English that you want to learn how to say in (the target language).

Accurately conjugate the verb "to be" (in target language).

Respond to the question by writing a complete sentence response (in the target language) on your whiteboards and holding them up.

1.) What do you write with?
2.) What do you eat with?
3.) What do you use to carry your books around?

Suggestions for Writing Your Own Mini Whiteboard Activators:

You will find that the Mini Whiteboard Activator can be used in a variety of ways, which is why they are many teachers' go-to Activators. Essentially any question you would ask a student to respond to on paper (that doesn't require an extensive response) can be used for a Mini Whiteboard Activator. Consider ways you can have students generate lists, draw symbols or simple images, or construct diagrams to show their understanding of your content.

YOUR TURN

Design Your Own Mini Whiteboard Activators

A Checklist for Designing Effective Activators:

☐ *Does the prompt support a specific learning outcome?*

☐ *Is the prompt engaging?* Can students respond without feeling anxious or uncomfortable? Do students have enough prior knowledge to feel competent in their responses? Will the prompt ignite curiosity, make content relevant, and challenge students to think at a high level?

☐ *Is the prompt crafted with invitational language that promotes exploration and reduces the need for certainty?* Invitational prompts might begin with "What might...?" "What are some of the...?" or "What is your hunch for why...?"

As students engage in physical movement associated with specific knowledge, they generate a mental image of that knowledge. As they make motions and talk about what they are doing, they encode information in their memory in multiple ways, helping them increase their understanding of concepts."

—Ceri B. Dean, Elizabeth Ross Hubbell, Howard Pitler and BJ Stone

Card Sorts

Students collaborate to sort, match or sequence cards with various content information.

Once you have tried Card Sorts you will understand immediately why teachers make the time to create them; even your most reluctant learners can't help themselves from diving in to examine the cards and start to sort them. The novelty and hands-on aspect of Card Sorts intrigues students and does wonders for keeping small groups focused and on task as they discuss and deliberate over the content. And physically moving the cards around has the added benefit of creating visual patterns that anchor concepts in students' memories.

> **Materials Tip:** For an easy way to create your own cards with text or images, create a two-column multi-row table in a Word document. Then input the card content, adjust the font size appropriately and print. The table lines will give you clear cutting lines to follow. Be sure to determine a way to keep card sets together and organized from class to class. Envelopes, zip-top bags, or a binder clip can be useful for this. If you are short on time, have students in your first class cut the cards for you. (Just make sure they are not in order on the page.) Consider laminating card sets you plan on using throughout the years. For inspiration, we have provided sample Card Sort sets for download at http://www.esrnational.org/activators.

What are the ways the Card Sort Activator supports the conditions for engagement?

- Garners **good will** by encouraging student voice
- Supports **participation** by providing verbal and nonverbal ways to think and participate
- Captures **attention** by incorporating manipulatives and an opportunity to interact with peers
- Increases **interest** by posing a challenge that incorporates elements of a game
- Fosters **effort** by providing opportunities for practice, feedback, and revision
- Creates **investment** by offering efficient ways to reflect on Classroom Expectations or Classroom Agreements

TIME: 10-15 MINUTES

TEACHER PREP LIST

- ❑ Select content for the Card Sort that is rich and substantive enough to encourage student deliberation over the best way to match or sort
- ❑ Create and cut a set of cards for each student group
- ❑ Display prompt and student directions
- ❑ If sorting cards into categories, write those categories on the board
- ❑ Decide how you will group students (pairs, trios, or small groups), making sure groups are small enough so everyone can participate effectively
- ❑ Prepare an answer key (optional)
- ❑ Timer

9

ACTIVATOR SNAPSHOT

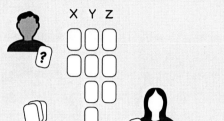

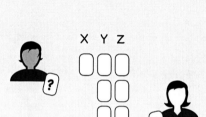

STUDENT DIRECTIONS

1. Spread the cards out on the desk so that everyone in your group can see them.

2. Group members examine all cards and discuss and determine how to sort them before moving any cards.

3. Group members work as a team to sort cards together, taking turns moving the cards.

SET UP THE ACTIVATOR

1. Explain the purpose of the Card Sort. You might say, "*I'm excited to give you the opportunity to do some problem solving together with a Card Sort Activator that will deepen your learning around _____.*"

2. Review student directions.

3. Communicate your expectations for handling the cards (e.g., returning them to an envelope afterwards, not folding them or writing on them.) You might say, "*Card Sorts take a lot of time to prepare so I need your help making sure the card sets stay together and separate from other sets of cards. When we are done I need you to count up all of your cards to make sure all are present and carefully return them to the plastic zip-top bag.*"

4. Distribute card sets to each pair, trio, or small group and ask students to leave the cards in the set (clip, envelope, zip-top bag) until you instruct them to begin.

MODEL AND TEACH

1. Gesture to the written prompt and say, *"In a moment, you will work in your pair or small groups to sort your cards the following way. You will have _____minutes and my expectation is that you will all be talking and thinking aloud as a team to complete this task."*

2. Model spreading the cards out, so that everyone in the pair, trio, or group can see them.

3. Do a Think Aloud to model how you would sort **one** of the cards according to the prompt. If sorting cards into categories, draw students' attention to the chart on the board that includes one example card correctly sorted and explain the rationale. Ask students what they noticed about sorting the cards.

4. Emphasize that this is an activity where they are required to talk to their partners. You might say, *"As I walk around the room, I am listening to hear each group discussing the cards and thinking out loud about how they are making decisions to sort them."*

PRACTICE AND ASSESS

1. Tell students how much time they will have to sort the cards, and invite them to begin.

2. Circulate, monitor, and support students' active participation and learning.

3. Since it can be challenging to check multiple groups for accuracy if they finish at the same time, you might want to prepare an answer key in advance that teams can use to check their work when they are done. If you do so, ask groups to select a team spokesperson for this purpose. Alternatively, you can circulate to check that each group has correctly matched the cards you know are most challenging.

4. When you see cards that are matched incorrectly, probe students to explain the reasons they sorted the way they did. If students have multiple mismatches, ask them if they would like help identifying the cards that are mismatched. If they agree, move those cards off to the side, offer a hint or tip, and invite them to try again with those cards.

5. Remind students of how much time is remaining.

6. When time is up, use a signal to get the group's attention and debrief by asking some of the following content and process questions:

Content questions
- What were some of the reasons for sorting the way you did?
- What questions do you have?

Process questions
- What was it like working in small groups to sort the cards?
- How does talking through things with partners impact your learning?

Thank students for their active participation, affirm understandings, and clear up any misconceptions that might have emerged.

9

TROUBLESHOOTING TIPS

- If students are struggling to match cards, that tells you that they are not solid on the information and need more teaching or modeling in order to be ready for this practice. In the moment, you can ask students to sort all of the cards they are unsure of into one column so you can scan the room and assess how to adjust your teaching.

- If groups are struggling to be productive, stop them and debrief in the moment. *"What is working? What are some of the things getting in the way of our productivity?"* You could also follow up by using the Group Behaviors Card Sort on pages 96–97 to establish or re-establish group work expectations.

- If one person takes over and starts sorting without consulting the group, ask the group to remix the cards and start over so that the whole group is involved and learning.

VARIATIONS AND EXTENSIONS

- Use the same cards for sorting in different ways: categorizing, matching, sequencing, labeling with arrow cards, and/or reviewing for an assessment.

- Have students create an annotated visual by arranging the cards in response to the prompt, taping or gluing the card arrangement to a piece of paper, and adding details, notes, arrows, illustrations, etc.

- Students can work in table groups to create a Card Sort for reviewing a unit concept or topic prior to an assessment. Students can then rotate tables to do all groups' Card Sorts to review and prepare for the assessment.

- Invite students who need extra practice or review to take a set of cards home with them to study.

- Have students create additional cards to complement those you used in class (i.e., images, examples, descriptors, quotes, etc.).

- Use these same cards in a Rotating Line-up or a Mix and Mingle to review for an assessment by giving each student one vocabulary or concept card to review with each talking partner.

Using Card Sorts to Create a High-Performing Community of Learners

For many students, Card Sorts provide just the right mix of novelty, challenge, and support. While Card Sorts are a fabulous tool to support content knowledge acquisition, they are just as effective for creating conditions that will support students being emotionally and socially engaged. Inviting students to use Emotion Words Cards to share how they feel about your subject based on their past experiences with it, communicates that you care about them as individuals, acknowledges that not everyone loves your discipline, and sets the stage for relational trust.

Using the Group Behaviors Card Sort to identify behaviors that "add to and subtract from the group" is a tried and true activity that efficiently gets students talking about what group behaviors they should be trying on and what behaviors they should try to minimize. The Card Sort allows them to talk about behaviors in a neutral way, and groups and teachers alike benefit from the hyper awareness of student behavior that follows.

Card Sort Examples for Creating a High-Performing Community of Learners

- Group Behaviors Cards: Sort the Group Behaviors Cards that add and subtract from the group. Then sort the behaviors in order from those you feel are most helpful to those you feel are most harmful to a group (see Group Behaviors Cards on pages 96–97).

- Emotions Cards: Give each group member a turn to sort cards and share aloud while sorting how they often feel, sometimes feel, and rarely feel about (subject area). Debrief with whole-group Wave around: "One way I often feel or sometimes feel about (subject area) is _____."

- Classroom Agreements Cards: Have students sort your Classroom Agreements into two columns: Consistently Upholding/Need to Work On. Note: This requires the teacher to create a Card Sort that includes the Classroom Agreements your group decided upon.

9

Example Card Sort

The group behavior cards found on the adjacent page can be used to support the development of Classroom Agreements. This card sort set can also be very useful at the beginning of a group project because it provides a safe forum for student groups to share what behaviors they value in their peers while also naming behaviors that harm a group's ability to be productive and positive. By providing a common language and definition for these behaviors, students are better equipped to self-reflect, set goals, and self-monitor around how they function in groups.

For a downloadable version of these cards, please visit http://www.esrnational.org/activators, where you will also find ready to print example card sorts for each of the content areas that we offer in this book, including:

- **Math:** Geometry (volume and surface areas of geometric solids)
- **Science:** Biology (cell organelles)
- **Social Studies:** Geography or Economics (demographic terminology)
- **English Language Arts:** Vocabulary (Latin word roots)
- **World Languages:** Spanish (thematic vocabulary)
- **Creating a High Performing Community of Learners** (emotion word cards)

Creating a High Performing Community of Learners: Group Behaviors Cards

Suggested directions:

1. Take turns reading each card aloud and sorting them into two piles based on if the behavior described would "add" or "subtract" from the energy or productivity of a group.

2. Work with your group to sort the behaviors in order from those you feel are most helpful to those you feel are most harmful to a group.

3. Self reflect and discuss with your group: which of the "adding" behaviors are strengths for you? Are there any "subtracting" behaviors you sometimes slip into? Which behavior would you like to increase or decrease? Which behaviors would you like to see more of when you are working in a group?

✂ —

Problem Solving

Asking questions, offering ideas, proposing next steps, experimenting, respectfully identifying off-track behaviors

Dominating

Telling others what to do, insisting their ideas are better than others', dominating the spotlight, and taking all of the credit

Organizing/Coordinating

Keeping the group on track, focusing on goals, monitoring resources, suggesting timelines, proposing fair division of the workload

Distracting

Talking about everything except the task at hand, fidgeting, making noises, telling jokes, calling attention to themselves and others

Seeking/Questioning

Identifying what information and resources are needed, doing research, connecting different ideas, asking related questions, offering perspectives to invite participation and thinking

Blocking

Rarely offering an idea, often finding flaws in others' ideas, disagreeing without listening carefully, playing the devil's advocate long after it's useful

Encouraging

Encouraging everyone's participation and thinking, praising specific efforts, staying positive and supportive

Withdrawing

Being consistently silent or out of the loop, not sharing ideas, not doing a fair share of the work, drifting along

Clarifying/Summarizing

Checking the groups' understanding, clearing up confusion, offering summaries

Doom-and-Glooming

Expecting the group to fail, arguing that plans and ideas won't work, saying that the group won't be able to accomplish the task, spreading a sour mood

9

Using Card Sorts to Support Learning in the Content Areas

Provide Opportunities to Practice Skills and Deepen Understanding: Card Sorts can be an effective way for students to learn foundational content. For example, if students in an algebra class repeatedly practice sorting examples into associative, commutative and distributive properties, the information will soon become automatic. Racing to match the correct cards adds a game element that infuses fun and excitement into an otherwise mundane memorization task. While Card Sorts can help students practice with basic facts or vocabulary that are foundational to deeper thinking, they can also be a tool for deep thinking and discussion. Determining the most significant event factoring into the start of World War I, for example, is a task that will force students to evaluate information, interpret cause and effect, make claims, and support them with evidence.

Support Formative Assessment: Circulating around the room while students are doing a Card Sort provides a visual snapshot of what they do and do not know. Card Sort Activators quickly allow you to see trends in the room and within groups, providing you with clear evidence of what concepts are tripping them up or causing confusion. In a class where students are matching economic terms with definitions and examples, a teacher can easily see what foundational terms are more or less confusing for students and immediately follow up with corrective feedback or a mini-lesson.

Prepare Students for Assessments: Cards that you create over the course of the unit can be brought back out to help students review prior to an assessment. You could have stations set up around the room before a mid-term assessment so students can practice matching vocabulary and images at one table, then practice using the correctly conjugated verbs at another table, and so on. At the end of a unit, you could also create different prompts and questions to push students to higher levels of thinking with the same cards they initially used for learning foundational knowledge. Having students create their own Card Sorts is another creative way to help them extend their learning and show evidence of their ability to apply their knowledge beyond the scope of your unit.

Math

Math Foundations
Match equivalencies (percentage, fraction, decimal).

Algebra
Sort examples into associative, commutative and distributive properties.

Geometry
Match each picture of a geometric solid with its correct name, volume and surface area formulas (images of geometric solids for this card sort are available online at http://www.esrnational.org/activators).

Science

Earth Science
Sort into renewable and non-renewable energy sources.

Biology
Match the cell organelles with their function, illustration, and city analogy (images of cell organelles for this card sort are available online at http://www.esrnational.org/activators).

Sequence steps and illustrations in mitosis and meiosis (different colored cards for each process).

Chemistry
Sort elements into metals, non-metals, and metalloids.

Physics
Sequence the cards in the order of the electromagnetic spectrum.

Social Studies

Geography
Match Trios: Country Economic and Developmental Indicator Terms + Definition + Examples (for example: GDP, Per Capita Income, etc.)

U.S. History
Categorize social, political, and economic effects of the Great Depression, then identify which three you feel had the greatest impact on American society.

9

World History

Sequence the events leading up to World War I in the order of greatest impact to least impact on the start of the war.

English Language Arts

Writing

Sort the transition words into categories: similarity, contrast, sequence, examples, effect, conclusion

Reading — Literature

Sequence five to seven key events in _____ .

Reading — Informational Texts

Sort claims that are supported by facts, reasons, and evidence and those that are not, in Winston Churchill's "Blood, Sweat and Tears" speech

Speaking and Listening

Sort qualities of debate vs. dialogue.

Language

Match Latin roots and with their meaning (images of Latin roots for this card sort are available online at http://www.esrnational.org/activators).

World Languages

Sort key vocabulary into themes: clothing, weather, food.

Sort correct conjugation of verb with appropriate sentences that have a blank space indicating a missing verb.

Match vocabulary to images.

Have students create their own Card Sorts using vocabulary related to the unit theme.

Suggestions for Writing Your Own Card Sort Activators

When considering designing Card Sorts for your units, think beyond terms and definitions. Because Cards Sorts take time to prepare, be sure you get your value out of all that cutting by focusing on essential content that you can use in more than one way over the course of your unit or course. You might try matching images with concepts. If there are categories of information in your unit or course, consider making category cards one color, and example cards another, so students can group multiple cards together based on characteristics.

9

YOUR TURN

Design Your Own Card Sorts Activators

Brain research tells us that when the fun stops, learning often stops too.
—Judy Willis

Toss One, Take One

Students write a response to a prompt on a small piece of paper, crumple it up and toss it to try to "make a basket," and then retrieve a classmate's anonymous response that they share aloud to the class.

This Activator, which can be done relatively quickly, is a big hit with middle and high school students. The novelty of crumpling up paper, the playfulness of trying to make a "basket" with it, followed by the opportunity to read another student's anonymous idea is the "perfect storm" for creating a classroom of engaged students.

What are the ways the Toss One, Take One Activator supports the conditions for engagement?

- Garners **good will** by allowing students to be known and heard
- Supports **participation** by offering a low risk and playful way for all students to share ideas and knowledge
- Captures **attention** by incorporating novelty and movement
- Increases **interest** by incorporating elements of a game
- Fosters **effort** by providing low-risk practice opportunities
- Supports **investment** by offering ways to reflect on Classroom Expectations and Classroom Agreements

TIME: 5–10 MINUTES

TEACHER PREP LIST

☐ Design an engaging prompt aligned to a learning outcome.

☐ Place a clean and empty container to use as the basket in the center of the room.

☐ Display the prompt and student directions.

☐ Half or quarter-size pieces of scrap paper.

☐ Timer

ACTIVATOR SNAPSHOT

STUDENT DIRECTIONS

1. Write your response to the prompt neatly on scrap paper (no names).

2. Crumple your paper into a ball. When I say "Go!" gently toss it to try and make a basket, and pay attention to where it lands.

3. Retrieve a paper ball (not your own).

4. Uncrumple the paper ball, review it silently, and be ready to read it aloud when it is your turn.

SET UP THE ACTIVATOR

1. Explain the purpose of using this Activator. You might say, "*Toss One, Take One is a fun way to get everyone's ideas and thinking in the room in a way that is both energizing and anonymous—which adds an element of mystery.*"

2. Review student directions.

MODEL AND TEACH

1. Model exactly how you would like students to crumple up the paper to ensure they do not make a paper ball no one can reopen.

2. Model tossing the paper gently to try and make a basket.

3. Ask students what they noticed about how you crumpled and tossed the paper, and establish your expectations.

PRACTICE AND ASSESS

1. Distribute a half- or quarter-size piece of scrap paper to each student.

2. Direct students to the prompt and let them know they have 90 seconds to respond to the question silently, neatly, and anonymously on their scrap paper. (No names, and legible so someone else can read it.)

3. Ask all students to crumple their paper into a ball. Remind them to be careful not to tear it or crumple it so tightly that no one will be able to open it back up.

4. Optional: Invite all students to stand and move to the periphery of the room and direct them to the basket you have placed in the middle of the room.

5. Remind them to throw the papers gently to try and make a basket. You might say, *"On the count of three, try to toss your paper ball gently into the "basket" and keep an eye on where it lands."* Count to three and watch the papers fly.

6. Use a signal to get the group's attention, and acknowledge how many papers made it into the basket. You will need to harness that energy to ensure on-task and productive thinking, so insist on silence before moving ahead with the Activator.

7. Tell students that when you say *"Go!"* they have 30 seconds to go and pick up someone else's piece of paper, return to their seat, and open it up and see what it says. Keep time to ensure a quick transition. (If a student happened to pick up their own paper, ask them to quickly switch with a neighbor.)

8. Use a signal to get the group's attention, and invite students to share out the responses on the paper they picked up, using a Wave or Popcorn format (Chapter 4). You might ask them to start with a common sentence stem such as, *"Someone in this room said/wrote/answered _____ ."* With a large class, you can first have students Turn and Talk to share what is on their paper, and then call on pairs to share one thing from either of their papers.

9. Depending upon the purpose, you may chart responses to capture answers or trends in thinking.

10. Debrief by asking some of the following content and process questions:

    ### Content questions
    - What are some things you heard that stood out to you?
    - What patterns did you notice in the responses?
    - What are some things you realized or are wondering about _____ ?

10

Process questions:

■ What do you think about Toss One, Take One? How did it affect the energy level in the room?

Thank students for their active participation, affirm understandings, and address any misconceptions that may have surfaced.

TROUBLESHOOTING TIPS

■ If students cannot read the handwriting on their paper, have them consult with another student.

■ If you are not getting high quality responses, you might collect a few exemplary responses and show them to students before repeating the Activator on another day.

VARIATIONS AND EXTENSIONS

■ If using Toss One, Take One on a regular basis, you can increase the competition aspect by dividing the room in half, having a basket for each side, and keeping a running score of papers that make it into the basket for each side.

■ Follow up the Toss One, Take One with a Turn and Talk to provide further opportunity for student discussion and processing.

■ If you are recording responses, you could follow up by identifying categories for responses or graphing the data.

Using Toss One, Take One to Create a High-Performing Community of Learners

Toss One, Take One offers a "cool" way for adolescents to participate authentically and share their perspectives in order to establish Classroom Agreements. The anonymity of this Activator provides a forum for students to speak freely about their needs as learners. Consider using it on a monthly or quarterly basis to provide a ritualized way for students to reflect on how they are living up to those Agreements.

Toss One, Take One is also a great way to ask students to reflect on their Habits of Learning or voice a strategy for improving academic performance. Students can benefit by hearing multiple ideas for how to improve their grade or performance and the power of a peer's suggestion is often more palatable and powerful for adolescent learners.

Toss One, Take One Examples for Creating a High-Performing Community of Learners

- What are some of the things that you need from your classmates to feel safe, comfortable, and ready to learn?

- What is one of our Group Agreements we are doing well with? What is one Group Agreement we are struggling with?

- What are two or three things you need to do to be successful in this class?

Using Toss One, Take One to Support Learning in the Content Areas

Generate Connections to Prior Knowledge: Toss One, Take One is an ideal way to assess and establish background knowledge. Asking students to share what they know or want to know on a topic is a typical way to start a unit, and Toss One, Take One provides a forum for low-risk participation with an added twist of novelty and fun. It also allows the teacher to clarify facts and tap into what students are curious about.

Provide Opportunities to Practice Skills and Deepen Understanding: Turning Toss One, Take One into a game with several questions can be a fun way to practice solving math equations, practice balancing chemical equations, or practice a variety of other skills. This injects a game-like aspect that brings enthusiasm for practice that you simply cannot get from a handout. Be sure to announce or display the correct answer and troubleshoot why some students might have not answered correctly in between each round, so students can receive immediate feedback and make necessary corrections for the next round.

In a math class, you also could provide students a problem that may be solved in multiple ways. Have students either individually or in partners solve the problem and crumple their paper and toss it at the basket. Then ask students to retrieve a different paper (Take One) and determine if they solved it the same way. Call on various pairs to both share out the answer and state the method that was used to solve the problem. You can either review these methods beforehand or see if these methods come out in students' responses. You might have students write on the board or use a document camera to show the various methods. Some debrief questions might include: *"Did you learn about a method that you hadn't used before? Might one of these methods be more accurate? More efficient? When would that be? What type of problem would make elimination the most efficient?"*

Conduct Formative Assessment: A Toss One, Take One prompt is one way to inject energy into a class while providing an opportunity to assess what students have learned or understood. In world languages, asking students to identify a word that is hard for them to pronounce provides the teacher with important information and gives the class an opportunity to practice saying the challenging words. Similarly, if the class spent Friday reviewing how to determine the reliability of a website in your English language arts class, you can kick off class on Monday with a Take One, Toss One that reveals what information "stuck" and what information needs to be reinforced.

Prepare Students for Assessments: Toss One, Take One is an effective way to help students prepare for written assessments. Let's imagine that students are writing an essay in response to a specific prompt such as "What were the important lessons of the Vietnam War?" You can use Toss One, Take One to help them prepare. Direct each student to write down one important idea or one important piece of evidence they think should be included in their essay. As each student shares out what was written on the paper they picked up, the class can identify it as a main idea or a piece of evidence. The subsequent class dialogue provides an opportunity to reinforce content as well as expectations for writing, such as always supporting main points with details and evidence.

Inject Relevance Into the Curriculum: As with most Activators that include an open-ended prompt, Toss One, Take One is also a creative way for teachers to push students to make real world connections to their content. For example, a biology teacher who asks students to identify what genetic disease they would study if they were a researcher invites students to connect the concept of DNA and genetics with the reality of genetic diseases like Down syndrome, Parkinson's disease, or sickle cell disease.

Math

Algebra

1.) Which method do you prefer for solving this system of linear equations algebraically? Show your work and explain your reasons for preferring this method.

$$\begin{cases} y = 2x + 4 \\ 3x + y = 9 \end{cases}$$

Team review competition: Divide class into two teams and give one team white paper and the other team colored paper. Show a problem on the board and have all students respond. Have all students shoot for the basket. Correct answers = 1 point, Correct answers in basket = 2 points

Geometry

Work with your partner to create a problem similar to the modeled problem. Sign your names on the problem.

Create an answer key on another slip of paper by completely solving the problem, showing all work (see example below). At the signal, toss your problem into the basket. Keep your answer key with you.

Take another pair's problem and collaboratively solve it with your partner.

Check your answer with the original answer key. For example, go up to the pair that created your problem and say, "We solved your problem. Can we see your answer key?"

Model Problem:
If these two figures are similar, find all of the missing dimensions.

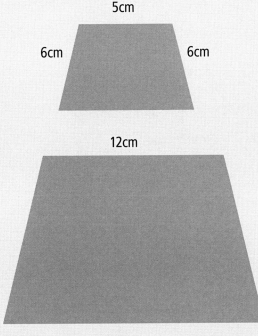

5cm

6cm   6cm

12cm

20cm

Model answer key:

I know from the problem that these two trapezoids are similar, which means that they are proportionate. If I divide 12cm/5cm I get 2.4, which means that the larger figure has a scale factor of 2.4. To get the diagonal sides of the larger trapezoid, multiply 6cm times 2.4 to get 14.4 cm. Lastly, to find the length of the base of the smaller trapezoid, divide 20cm by 2.4 to get 8 1/3 cm.

10

Science

Earth Science
What causes the phases of the moon?

Biology
If you were a genetics researcher, what would you study and why?

Chemistry
You buy a helium balloon on a cold winter day. You take it outside. What happens to the balloon and why?

Physics
Why do boats float?

Social Studies

U.S. History
Based on the primary sources we just reviewed, was Christopher Columbus a hero or a villain? Justify your response with at least one piece of evidence.

World History
What do you know or want to know about the Middle East?

Identify one way the ways the Scramble for Africa impacted the continent and its people in the short term and one way it impacted them in the long term.

Economics
What is a specific question you have about the concept of supply and demand?

Government
What is one right guaranteed under the Constitution you would be willing to give up? What is one you would fight to protect?

English Language Arts

Writing
What are some ways you can determine the credibility of a website?

Reading — Literature
What's a headline or tweet of seven words or less that captures the essence of the conflict between Troy and Cory in Act I, Scene 3 of *Fences*?

Reading — Informational Texts
Was learning how to read a blessing or a curse for Frederick Douglass? Why?

Speaking and Listening
What was one thing many people agreed on during the discussion? What was one thing some people disagreed about?

Language
Use the context of the sentence to determine the meaning of the italicized word. Explain your thinking.

World Languages

(In target language) I am a girl/boy, I am wearing (color). I have (color) hair. Guess who I am.

(In target language) Write a sentence using the new vocabulary from today's lesson.

(In target language) What is one word that is challenging for you to pronounce?

Suggestions for Writing Your Own Toss One, Take One Activators:

Any prompt that can be answered with a one or two sentence response could be suitable for a quick Toss One, Take One. This Activator is best suited for a question that is open ended or has multiple possible answers, otherwise students will get impatient with hearing the same response repeated 35 times. Alternatively, it is also a good way to game up skills practice. Consider using Toss One, Take One when you want to have students brainstorm, voice their opinions, describe how they arrived at an answer, or practice solving problems in a game-like format.

YOUR TURN

Design Your Own Toss One Take One Activators

A Checklist for Designing Effective Activators:

☐ *Does the prompt support a specific learning outcome?*

☐ *Is the prompt engaging?* Can students respond without feeling anxious or uncomfortable? Do students have enough prior knowledge to feel competent in their responses? Will the prompt ignite curiosity, make content relevant, and challenge students to think at a high level?

☐ *Is the prompt crafted with invitational language that promotes exploration and reduces the need for certainty?* Invitational prompts might begin with "What might…?" "What are some of the…?" or "What is your hunch for why…?"

Vision trumps all other senses.

—John J. Medina

Image Cards

Students respond to a prompt by selecting an image that represents their thinking.

Very few strategies bring a hush over the room and immediate interest and focus the way a smattering of Image Cards laid out across the floor or a table does. Students' eyes are drawn instantly to the colorful pictures, resulting in their curious expressions and comments. We often see groups impatient for the bell to ring and signal the start of class, eager to find out what their teacher is up to. Image Cards are a hit with all grade levels. The power of the visual and the large variety of choices make it one of the more popular Activators. When students represent knowledge non-linguistically, they tap "into [their] natural tendency for visual image processing, which helps them construct meaning of relevant content and skills and have better capacity to recall it later." (Dean et al., 2012) And using images can be particularly helpful for English Language Learners and Special Education students in making abstract ideas concrete (Hill & Flynn, 2006; Jordan, 2013).

> **Materials Tip:** We have provided a sample Image Card set for download at http://www.esrnational.org/activators; all images in this sample set may be used free of copyright restriction. You can also create your own original set using clip art, photos, or other images. Consider laminating the Image Cards that you plan on using throughout the years.

What are the ways the Image Cards Activator supports the conditions for engagement?

- Garners **good will** by providing materials that support different types of learners
- Supports **participation** by offering visual support for thinking
- Captures **attention** by fostering anticipation, and incorporating visuals
- Increases **interest** by generating curiosity and by injecting novelty and relevance by allowing students to construct meaning for themselves
- Fosters **effort** because there is no "right" answer
- Supports **investment** by offering creative and low-risk ways to reflect on Classroom Expectations and Classroom Agreements

TIME: 10-15 MINUTES

TEACHER PREP LIST

- ❏ Cut out Image Cards. We suggest laminating your Image Cards and keeping them in a large envelope to ensure they will last from year to year
- ❏ Identify a space large enough to spread out cards on the floor or on a table so that students can form a standing circle around the cards. This enables students to view all of the images easily
- ❏ Design an engaging prompt aligned to a learning outcome
- ❏ Display the prompt and student directions
- ❏ Select an image to use for modeling
- ❏ Timer

ACTIVATOR SNAPSHOT

STUDENT DIRECTIONS

1. Scan the images and select one that represents your thinking about

   _____ .

2. Move to pick up the image.

3. Hold up your image and be ready to explain why you selected it.

SET UP THE ACTIVATOR

1. Explain the purpose of the Activator. You might say, *"We're going to do an Activator that will push your thinking by asking you to make connections between _____ and an image. We call this symbolic thinking, which is a high-level skill. I'm confident you will maximize your ability to think symbolically with more and more practice."*

2. Invite students to start scanning the images with their eyes, but leave the cards in place until you are completely done with the directions.

3. Review student directions. Gesture to the written prompt and say, *"In a moment, I will ask you to pick an image that _____"*

MODEL AND TEACH

1. Model moving and selecting an image in response to a prompt that is different than the one you are offering students. In this way, your model will not influence students' selections.

2. Hold up the image so everyone can see it, and explain how it represents your thinking about _____ . Modeling gives you a chance to provide a concrete example of what symbolic thinking looks like. It also ensures students do not just pick a card with a picture of something they happen to like, forcing them to scramble mentally in the middle of the Activator to try to figure out a way to associate it with the prompt.

3. Ask students what they noticed about selecting and sharing an image.

4. Acknowledge that learners will approach this task in different ways. Some students might start by intuitively selecting an image and then figure out what their thinking is behind this choice; others might start with an idea first and find an image that represents this.

PRACTICE AND ASSESS

1. Tell students they have 90 seconds of silent think time to come up with their answer and after the 90 seconds you will instruct them to pick up their card.

2. After 90 seconds, invite students to move calmly to pick up the card they have selected.

3. If more than one student selects the same Image Card, you can either have them share it by moving and standing next to the other person in the circle, or they can pass the Image Card to the other person when it is time for them to share.

4. With groups smaller than 20, invite a volunteer to start and ask the person to their right if they would mind going next. Let the group know that you will proceed clockwise until everyone has a chance to share. Thank individual students after they share. Support students, as needed by asking questions that

help them clarify or elaborate on their responses, for example, "*Jasmin, please talk a little more about the connection between an anchor and the character of Rose in* Fences." With larger groups, start first with a Turn and Talk (Chapter 4) so that each student can share out their response. Circulate, monitor, and support students' active participation and learning. Then bring the class back together and draw eight to ten names using a random "cold call" strategy, and ask those students to share out their thinking with the group.

5. Thank students for their creative thinking and ask for several volunteers to help pick up all the cards and return them to you.

6. Debrief with the class by asking a few of the following content and process questions:

Content questions
- What patterns did you notice in the responses?
- What response helped you understand or think about _____ differently?

Process questions
- What surprised you?
- How does thinking symbolically or hearing other people think this way help you?

Thank students for their active participation, affirm understandings, and clear up any misconceptions that might have emerged.

TROUBLESHOOTING TIPS
- If students struggle with symbolic thinking they might need more examples of what it looks like and sounds like to make analogies. Essentially, you are asking them to consider the characteristics of something and then determine if it shares those characteristics with something else or with themselves. Consider asking student to brainstorm characteristics, qualities, or key components of a concept first as a group before having them select cards.

- Another way to step into this type of thinking is to limit the options and break down the thinking. Are You More Like (Chapter 14) does this with two items. Depending upon how it is used, Four (or more) Corners can also require this same kind of thinking with a limited number of items. Scaffolding with these two Activators will help your students build the thinking skills necessary for Image Cards.

VARIATIONS AND EXTENSIONS
- In place of using actual Image Cards, you can create a digital image collage and project for students to see. (Go to http://www.esrnational.org/activators to download a sample digital image collage.)

- Use cards with smaller table groups instead of the whole class by creating multiple sets of a limited number of Image Cards, or dividing up the Image Cards among the table groups. Make sure each group has enough cards to increase choice (if there are four students in a group, consider having at least seven to eight cards)

- To practice listening and paraphrasing skills, have students do a Turn and Talk and share with a partner first, and then have them share out what their partner said.

- Have students search the Internet for additional images that relate to your content or unit to incorporate into your image collection.

- Have students create an annotated image collage to represent and explain key concepts from your unit or course.

Using Image Cards to Create a High-Performing Community of Learners

Being known and knowing others is an important step for building trust in a classroom environment—one of the key ingredients in creating a High-Performing Community of Learners. Image Cards are a great way for students to open up and learn about each other in a low-threat way. Students who might be uncomfortable with the request to share something about who they are respond with eagerness when they are presented with a multitude of colorful images that help spark their thinking. It also helps some students feel safer because this Activator allows them to refer to the image versus talking about themselves; thus the Image Card serves as a buffer for those students who need one as they work towards getting more comfortable with the group.

Because Image Cards are so well received by students, they lead to a wide variety of thoughtful responses. This offers a unique way to generate Classroom Agreements. Students can select an image to reflect on what they need to feel comfortable and able to learn in the classroom. Image Cards can similarly be used to help classes and groups revisit agreements to check in on what they are appreciating, noticing, or needing to change in order to be productive and engaged in learning. This type of reflection is invaluable for creating a High-Performing Community of Learners, and yet responses to the prompt might be simplistic or nonexistent without the cards to stimulate ideas.

Image Card Examples for Creating a High-Performing Community of Learners

- What image represents something about who you are or what you like to do?
- What image represents one way you feel about (insert course subject)?
- What image represents something you need to do/have/be in order to engage in learning and be productive in class?
- What image represents something you appreciated about working with your group on the project?

Using Image Cards to Support Learning in the Content Areas

Generate Connections to Prior Knowledge: It is likely that the majority of your students will be visual learners, and that is because your students have grown up in a largely visual world and have well-honed visual skills. They expect information to come with pictures, illustrations, and graphics, which is why students are so receptive to Image Card Activators. The sheer variety of images included in this book will also support divergent thinking, which makes Image Cards a great tool for activating background knowledge and making connections to your content. Asking students to select a card that represents something they already know about a subject or topic, such as Africa, can be a great way to conduct a brainstorm and help you pre-assess student knowledge or even identify preconceptions.

Provide Opportunities to Practice Skills and Deepen Understanding: When students connect their knowledge to an image—and hear their classmates do the same—it helps them retain information, and more importantly supports deep understanding. For example, students will be more able to deeply understand literary themes in a novel after they have spent time exploring the character of the protagonist by connecting images to his physical, social, intellectual, and emotional characteristics.

Support Formative Assessment: Asking students to pick a card that represents something they have learned about a topic is a creative way to conduct formative assessment. As you facilitate, you can punctuate critical points and insert probing questions that push students to clarify their understandings—to the benefit of all of their classmates. For example, if a student mistakenly provides erroneous information about the concept you are asking students to select an image for, you can intervene, reiterate your mantra that "mistakes help us learn" and clarify the inaccuracy.

Prepare Students for Assessments: Image Cards can provide a forum for pushing students to be introspective about their own performance in order to prepare for—or fine-tune—a final assessment. Asking students to pick an image that reflects one way they are going to revise an essay is a creative way for them to reflect and begin forming an action plan for revising their writing. Hearing their classmates' ideas will help all students by exposing them to a variety of ways to improve their essay.

Math

Mathematics
In a math class, we recommend using these cards to support students' Habits of Learning as a better fit than content connections.

Science

Earth Science
Pick a card that represents something you have learned about oceans.

Biology
Pick a card that represents the process of natural selection.

Chemistry
Pick a card that represents one of the properties of water.

Physics
Pick a card that represents one of Newton's Laws of Motion.

Social Studies

Geography
Pick a card that represents one of the elements of culture.

U.S. History
Pick a card that represents an aspect of U.S. culture or politics during the Roaring Twenties.

World History
Pick a card that represents something you know about Africa.

Psychology
Pick a card that represents one of the seven approaches to psychology.

11

English Language Arts

Writing
Pick a card that represents one way you plan to revise the first draft of your memoir.

Reading — Literature
Pick a card that represents one of Walter's character traits in *Raisin in the Sun*.

Reading — Informational Text
Pick a card that represents a central idea in The Gettysburg Address.

Speaking and Listening
Pick a card that represents a key idea from your literature circle's discussion of _____ .

Language
Pick a card that represents a connotation of the word _____ .

World Languages

Select an image that represents something you like and say in target language: I like _____ .

Student: Hold up an image card and say (In target language) What is/how do you say_____? Teacher: (in target language) That is a _____ .

Pick any card and be prepared to point out colors in the image.

Suggestions for Writing Your Own Image Card Activators

While it does take time and resources to download, print, cut, and laminate our Image Card set, if you use them regularly it is well worth the effort and students never tire of them. English teachers might consider supplementing our Image Cards with images of the cover of the novels students will read over the course of the year or novels they have read in past years. Science teachers might include images of scientific tools. We've also worked with world language departments that have pooled together their time and resources to create a different set of Image Cards for each of their themed units, enabling them to each have an Image Card set to represent key vocabulary words.

YOUR TURN

Design Your Own Image Card Activators

11

A Checklist for Designing Effective Activators:

☐ *Does the prompt support a specific learning outcome?*

☐ *Is the prompt engaging?* Can students respond without feeling anxious or uncomfortable? Do students have enough prior knowledge to feel competent in their responses? Will the prompt ignite curiosity, make content relevant, and challenge students to think at a high level?

☐ *Is the prompt crafted with invitational language that promotes exploration and reduces the need for certainty?* Invitational prompts might begin with "What might...?" "What are some of the...?" or "What is your hunch for why...?"

Cognitive psychologists widely accept...the adolescent's central developmental need...to argue in ways that make adults listen.

—Barbara Cervone and Kathleen Cushman

Opinion Continuum

Students take a position along a continuum to express their opinions regarding a controversial statement.

Opinion Continuum is a hit with adolescents who naturally gravitate towards controversy. Because students enjoy responding to questions that have no right answer, they are eager to take a stand in this Activator that acknowledges and welcomes multiple perspectives. This Activator involves movement, respects student voice, and is highly visual, which helps students to see the range of perspectives in the room.

What are the ways the Opinion Continuum Activator supports the conditions for engagement?

- Garners **good will** by honoring diverse points of view
- Supports **participation** by structuring a way for all students to share their opinions
- Captures **attention** by incorporating movement and providing an audience for students' responses
- Increases **interest** by putting controversial topics front and center
- Fosters **effort** by providing opportunities for practice and feedback
- Supports **investment** by offering ways to reflect on Classroom Expectations and Classroom Agreements

TIME: 15-20 MINUTES

TEACHER PREP LIST

- ❑ Design an engaging prompt aligned to a learning outcome that will evoke a range of responses
- ❑ Identify a space where students can line up
- ❑ Post two signs on opposite ends of the lineup area: "Strongly Agree" and "Strongly Disagree"
- ❑ Display prompt and student directions
- ❑ Index cards, sticky notes, scrap paper, or student notebooks
- ❑ Timer

ACTIVATOR SNAPSHOT

STUDENT DIRECTIONS

1. Read the prompt and jot down your opinion along with two or three supporting reasons on a sticky note/index card/scrap paper/in your notebook.

2. At the signal, take your sticky note/index card/scrap paper/notebook, and position yourself along the imaginary line based upon your opinion.

3. Turn and Talk to a partner about why you're standing where you are.

SET UP THE ACTIVATOR

1. Explain the purpose of the Activator. You might say, *"The Activator we're about to do will give you a chance to practice supporting your point of view about _____ . As you listen carefully to your classmates' opinions, you'll also practice an important skill for college, careers, and life—analyzing multiple perspectives. And because you'll be on your feet, your brain is more apt to pay attention and remember information and ideas."*

2. Review student directions.

3. Draw students' attention to two signs posted on opposite sides of the room labeled "Strongly Agree" and "Strongly Disagree." Ask students to imagine there is an imaginary line that runs from one sign to the other. Tell students you will read a statement and they will be asked to position themselves at some place along the imaginary line or continuum that represents their response.

MODEL AND TEACH

1. Model using a different statement than the one students will respond to. Jot down your opinion and two or three supporting reasons on the board. Explain that making some notes prior to getting up will help them anchor their thinking while talking to a peer.

2. Model where you might place yourself along the continuum based upon your opinion by doing a Think Aloud. Debrief by asking students what they noticed.

PRACTICE AND ASSESS

1. Show a statement and read it aloud. Have students jot down their opinions and some supporting reasons on an index card or sticky note prior to getting up.

2. Invite students to move to a place on the continuum that reflects their response.

3. Ask students to Turn and Talk (Chapter 4) for two minutes with someone nearby about their reasons for standing where they are.

4. Circulate to monitor that everyone is paired up, and let students know when there is one minute remaining. If the number of students is uneven, some can form trios instead of pairs.

5. Use a signal to get the group's attention, and ask students from different places along the continuum to share out some of their reasons for their position.

6. Explain that students can move at any point along the continuum in response to something that they heard a peer say.

7. Paraphrase and ask questions to help students elaborate or clarify their responses.

8. Debrief by asking the class a few of the following content and process questions:

Content questions

- What are one or two things a peer said that stood out to you?
- To what extent did your thinking about _____ deepen or shift as a result of participating in this Activator?
- What are some things you realized or are wondering about _____ ?

Process questions

- What did you like/dislike about this Activator?
- What are some reasons for hearing multiple perspectives?
- What are some situations when it might be helpful to shift your position after listening to someone else's perspective?

Thank students for their active participation, affirm understandings, and clear up any misconceptions that might have emerged.

TROUBLESHOOTING TIPS

- If your room is too small or you have fixed equipment, consider a secluded hallway to do the Activator.
- If students are challenged in supporting their opinions, use a Turn and Talk (Chapter 4) Activator to have pairs brainstorm possible reasons for both opinions and chart these up prior to doing an Opinion Continuum Activator. Alternatively, use a Card Sort Activator (Chapter 9) and provide students with reasons that support positions at both ends of the continuum, and students can sort these prior to engaging in the Opinion Continuum Activator.

VARIATIONS AND EXTENSIONS

- Place signs in four corners of the room: Strongly Agree, Agree, Strongly Disagree, Disagree. Ask students to move to a corner of the room that represents their response to a statement.
- Use a Turn and Talk (Chapter 4) or Popcorn (Chapter 4) Activator format to respond to an Opinion Continuum statement.
- Close by asking students from opposite sides of the spectrum to summarize the main points presented by the other side.
- Follow up by asking students to write a brief reflection on how their thinking deepened or shifted as a result of participating in the Activator. For example, *"Before, I thought _____ . Now, I'm thinking _____ because _____ ."* Or, they could write a paragraph with reasons that support their position.

12

Using Opinion Continuum to Create a High-Performing Community of Learners

Opinion Continuum is a way to foster Trust and Belonging by honoring different learning styles. For example, a geometry teacher might ask students to take a stand in response to the statement: *"The best way to solve a proof is to just jump in and get started."* In doing so, the teacher creates a safe space by affirming the idea that learners approach problem solving in multiple ways. This Activator also helps students learn about each other in ways that can help them work together effectively. At the same time, the teacher gathers critical information about students that can lead to differentiating instruction as well as configuring groupings for particular learning tasks.

Opinion Continuum is also a forum for student voice around Classroom Expectations and Classroom Agreements. In a language arts classroom where students have recently started interrupting and talking over one another, a teacher might ask students to position themselves along the Continuum in response to the following statement: *"We've been living up to the Classroom Agreement about letting people finish what they're saying before speaking."* This would provide an opportunity for students to self-assess and use evidence to support their position. It can then lead to problem solving around ways the class can get back on track with this agreement.

Opinion Continuum Examples for Creating a High-Performing Community of Learners

- I'm interested in a future career that involves science/math/writing/working with people from other cultures.

- When people collaborate, they think smarter and can accomplish more.

- We've been living up to the classroom agreement about letting people finish what they're saying before speaking.

- The best way to write an essay/solve a math problem/complete a science lab is to just jump in and begin.

Using Opinion Continuum to Support Learning in the Content Areas

Generate Connections to Prior Knowledge: Before reading Dr. Martin Luther King's *Letter from Birmingham Jail*, a language arts teacher might inject controversy and encourage student voice by asking students to respond to the following statement: *Citizens have a moral obligation to disobey unjust laws.* Getting students on their feet to engage with the text's central idea prior to reading prepares students for an active encounter with Dr. King's argument.

Provide Opportunities to Practice Skills and Deepen Understandings: Comparing different solution methods in an algebra class deepens students' understandings of each one. Opinion Continuum is an energizing way to engage students around whether they think it is more efficient to solve a problem using the substitution or the elimination method. Students who are unsure can be invited to stay in the middle of the continuum and hear from both sides. After turning and talking to their partners, students from different ends of the continuum can show their work on the board/overhead/document camera to convince those in the middle. In this way, more introverted students deepen their understanding through listening to peers while more extroverted students benefit from being able to convince others of the efficiency of their chosen method.

Provide Opportunities for Formative Assessment: A world history teacher might use Opinion Continuum to assess students' understanding of primary source documents they've read regarding the dropping of the atomic bomb in World War II by providing the following prompt: *"The U.S. was justified in using atomic weapons on Japan during World War II."* As the students share their responses, the teacher can probe for understanding and encourage students to support ideas with textual evidence. By hearing and questioning their peers' responses, students have the opportunity to deepen, clarify, or make a shift in their thinking. After listening for ways students use the documents to support their positions, the teacher can draw their attention to evidence they may have overlooked or that presented challenges for them.

Prepare Students for Assessments: Towards the end of a biology unit on genetics when students are preparing to write an essay, a teacher might use this Activator and provide the following prompt: *"Genetically modifying foods is a good idea."* By talking with their peers, students are testing out the extent to which they have reasons and examples to support their claim sufficiently. As well, immediate teacher feedback while students are rehearsing their ideas increases the opportunity for success on the end-of-unit assessment.

Inject Relevance into the Curriculum: Opinion Continuum makes connections to the world beyond the classroom, which can increase motivation within the classroom. For example, an Earth science teacher might open up her unit on the Earth-Moon system with the following statement: *"Private companies should take people to the moon."* Students who might have glazed over at the mention of "Earth-Moon system" are now intrigued by the idea that people would actually pay money to go to the moon, so they start to ask themselves questions that create interest in the unit: *"People want to travel there—I wonder what it's like? How long would it take? How far is it? What's the weather like? What would I need to pack?"*

12

Math

Algebra

The substitution method is more efficient than the elimination method to solve this system of equations:

$$\begin{cases} y = 2x + 4 \\ 3x + y = 9 \end{cases}$$

Geometry

Figure B holds more water than Figure A.

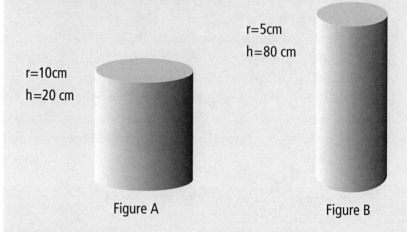

r=10cm
h=20 cm

r=5cm
h=80 cm

Figure A   Figure B

Science

Earth Science

Private companies should be able to take people to the moon.

Biology

Genetically modifying foods is a good idea.

Chemistry

There is no proof of global warming.

Physics

A larger ball will roll down a hill faster than a smaller ball.

Social Studies

U.S. History
Congress should pass the current immigration reform bill.

Economics
A free market system is only good to the wealthy and the middle class.

Government
The electoral college system should be eliminated and U.S. presidents should be elected by popular vote.

World History
The U.S. was justified in using atomic weapons on Japan during World War II.

English Language Arts

Writing
Teenagers should be allowed to vote.

Reading – Literature
The novel *The Hunger Games* is better than the film.

Reading – Informational Texts
Citizens have a moral obligation to disobey unjust laws.

Speaking and Listening
The president offered sound arguments in his demand for a vote on gun control in his State of the Union address.

Language
The best way to figure out the meaning of a word is to look it up.

12

World Languages

Ninety percent of communication is body language.

Your language shapes how you think.

It would be better if everyone in the world spoke the same language.

Suggestions for Writing Your Own Opinion Continuum Activators:

Review your unit with an eye towards learning outcomes that tap into adolescents' attraction to controversy. Where might there be opportunities for students to discuss issues that don't have just one answer? For an added motivational bonus, think about ways you can design compelling statements that link learning outcomes to your students' lives or larger societal issues. If students are writing an argumentative essay in a unit, you might design an Opinion Continuum Activator prompt as a way for students to rehearse and deepen their arguments prior to or during the writing process.

YOUR TURN

Design Your Own Opinion Continuum Activators

A Checklist for Designing Effective Activators:

☐ *Does the prompt support a specific learning outcome?*

☐ *Is the prompt engaging?* Can students respond without feeling anxious or uncomfortable? Do students have enough prior knowledge to feel competent in their responses? Will the prompt ignite curiosity, make content relevant, and challenge students to think at a high level?

☐ *Is the prompt crafted with invitational language that promotes exploration and reduces the need for certainty?* Invitational prompts might begin with "What might...?" "What are some of the...?" or "What is your hunch for why...?"

12

Movement anchors thought.

—CARLA HANNAFORD

Four (or more) Corners

Students respond to a prompt by selecting
and moving to the "corner" option
that best matches their thinking or interest.

Four (or more) Corners is an Activator that has been around for quite some time. Its staying power can be attributed to its flexibility and simplicity. Because Four (or more) Corners requires a modest amount of movement and we consider it a relatively easy Activator to facilitate, it is also an ideal choice for teachers who are looking to begin incorporating more student movement into their lessons.

What are the ways the Four (or more) Corner Activator supports the conditions for engagement?

- Fosters **good will** by inviting all voices into the room
- Supports **participation** by creating a low-risk way for everyone to simultaneously respond to a content question
- Captures **attention** by incorporating movement and novelty
- Increases **interest** by creating an opportunity to voice an opinion
- Supports **effort** by welcoming student voice and the sharing of a variety of responses and perspectives

TEACHER PREP LIST

- ❑ Post numbers around the periphery of the room to indicate the "corner" locations

- ❑ Design an engaging prompt aligned to a learning outcome

- ❑ Display the prompt and each of the corner options as well as student directions. For larger classes consider a larger number of "corners," or two sets of "four corners" for each side of the room to help ensure corner groups are not too large

- ❑ Develop and display sentence starters

- ❑ Timer

ACTIVATOR SNAPSHOT

STUDENT DIRECTIONS

1. Do a Quick Jot listing two or three reasons for choosing the corner you will move to.

2. At the signal, take your Quick Jot and move to the corner.

3. At your corner, Turn and Talk to a partner about your choice.

13

SET UP THE ACTIVATOR

1. Explain your purpose for using the Activator. You might say, *"This Activator is designed to inject energy into today's lesson by getting us all up and moving. And because it requires you to make a choice and defend that choice with one or more of your classmates, it will also help you remember important content information."*

2. Review student directions.

3. Review the posted prompt and ask students to consider the four (or more) optional responses.

4. Explain to students that they will be moving to the "corner" of their choice momentarily and will be expected to share their thinking in pairs or trios with others who gather in the same corner. Alert them to be prepared to share some of their thinking with the entire class.

MODEL AND TEACH

1. Model physically moving to a corner choice. Depending upon the type of prompt, you might also show some sentence starters that students could use to jump-start their thinking, for example: *"The main reason I choose this corner is because _____ . I was debating between _____ and _____ , but chose this corner because _____ ."*

2. For prompts that require students to explain the rationale for their choice, model how you expect them to jot down their response on something they can take with them as they move—a notebook page, scrap piece of paper, or sticky note. Having students write down their responses to the prompt prior to asking them to move to the corner allows them an opportunity to "rehearse" and feel prepared to share their thinking aloud with a peer. It is also a way to make sure students go to the corner that represents their individual thinking or interests instead of being tempted to follow their friends to a corner.

PRACTICE AND ASSESS

1. Provide students with silent think-time to determine which corner they will go to.

2. Invite all students to stand. Explain that when you say *"Go!"* they will have 30 seconds to quickly move to their corner choice and find their talking partners. Say *"Go!"* and begin.

3. Circulate to monitor and facilitate efficient student movement, active participation, and learning. *"I want to hear you identify at least two reasons why you chose this corner and why you intentionally didn't choose some of the other options."*

4. Use a signal to get the whole group's attention when you are ready to begin the debrief. While students are still standing in corners, call on someone from each corner to share out their reasoning. Continue to debrief the Activator by asking the class some of the following content and process questions:

Content questions

- What is one thing you learned or realized as a result of listening to the thinking of other groups?
- What are you wondering about _____ ?
- Having heard the other groups' reasons, are any of you convinced to move? If so, explain how your thinking changed.

Process questions

- What did you like or dislike about this Activator?
- How did having to choose between four (or more) options impact your thinking?

Thank students for their active participation, affirm understandings, and clear up any misconceptions that might have emerged.

TROUBLESHOOTING TIPS

- Be sure you teach, model, and practice several Turn and Talks prior to using this Activator in order to ensure students feel comfortable and able to engage in a short dialogue with a partner.

- Consider stepping through the instructions more slowly and explicitly the first few times you use this Activator. For example, you might pause the class when they get to the corner and provide more specific instructions such as, *"Turn and face a partner or form a trio if you have an odd number at your corner. Take turns explaining at least two reasons why you chose to move to your corner."*

- If you anticipate a group might be in trouble or see them struggling, move in immediately and orchestrate the grouping of partners or re-direct students who might have gotten off track by asking a question like *"What were some of your reasons for moving to this corner?"*

VARIATIONS AND EXTENSIONS

- Instead of each corner simply representing one of the possible responses to the prompt, posting quotes or images or placing an object or artifact at each corner for students to explore and learn from is a great way to enhance this Activator.

- Consider having an "other" corner choice to encourage divergent and creative thinking.

13

Using Four (or more) Corners to Create a High-Performing Community of Learners

Four (or more) Corners Activators are a great way to promote a variety of expectations for student collaboration and work. If a teacher asks students to stand by the corner representing how they will prepare for an important assessment, students who don't usually prepare for assessments because they don't know how, or have ineffective work or study habits, have an opportunity to explore a variety of ways they can step up their effort. They get to see that there are options, such as studying with a friend, making flash cards, reviewing their notes, or anticipating the essay question that could help them be successful. It also pushes them to be metacognitive by asking them to self-reflect and make a choice about which one would be most useful. This important skill is reinforced even more as students hear from their classmates how each of them will tailor their effort to their own needs in order to prepare for an important assessment.

This Activator is also a natural fit for having students reflect on the Habits of Learning you want to reinforce. Identify four to six Habits of Learning (see Appendix 3 for Habits of Learning), post them around your room, and invite students to reflect on them and identify one Habit they would like to work on improving. When students are regularly asked to be mindful of these Habits, they are able to practice the important skills of self-reflection and goal setting. Naming each Habit and giving students an opportunity to talk about them will also help students develop an academic mindset and give them an opportunity to get ideas from peers and feel inspired to tackle an area that challenges them.

Four (or more) Corner Examples for Creating a High-Performing Community of Learners

What behavior do you think is most valuable for productive group work?

- Asking Questions
- Problem Solving
- Organizing
- Encouraging

What is the most important thing for you to do tonight to make sure you are prepared for tomorrow's end-of-unit assessment?

- Get a good night's sleep and eat a healthy breakfast
- Review my notes with a study partner
- Make flash cards and self-quiz
- Complete the study guide and practice problems
- Anticipate possible essay questions and brainstorm outlines
- Other

Which Habit of Learning is a strength of yours, or which Habit of Learning is something you would like to work on during the next unit?

- Working cooperatively with others.
- Attempting each part of the question, task, assignment or test.
- Handling mistakes, setbacks, anger and frustration constructively.
- Using positive, non-aggressive language to express myself, ask for help and get what I need.
- Demonstrating curiosity and asking questions to probe for deeper understanding.

Using Four (or more) Corners to Support Learning in the Content Areas

Activate Prior Knowledge and Introduce Content: When quotes, images, objects, or artifacts are part of the Four (or more) Corners, this Activator is a novel way to introduce a new topic and connect to or create concrete background knowledge. Students starting a new unit on the 1920s in a U.S. history class can immediately see from the "corner" options that there were a variety of social changes that took place during this decade. Intriguing photographs with bold headings of 1920s automobiles, women's clothing, household advertisements, movie stars, and prohibition in action will entice students to explore the changes that were taking place in this long-ago decade, and make connections to today's social issues.

Practice Skills and Deepen Understanding: Developing skills takes time and effort and Four (or more) Corners is one way to provide an injection of interest, movement, and collaboration to help students stay motivated through the necessary practice. In fact, recent studies have found that "personalized math problems not only made it easier for students to understand what was being asked, but also helped boost the confidence of students who may have been intimidated by the subject" (Sparks, 2012). An algebra Four (or more) Corners Activator where students get to choose the corner with a word problem related to a topic they love (e.g., money, jewelry, cars, music, etc.) provides an opportunity for all students to practice the same necessary skills, but in the context of their own interests, providing differentiated support.

Review Prior to an Assessment: A simple but effective way to provide differentiated review time for an assessment is to have the "corner" options represent major concepts from your unit. A world language class where students choose a corner for reviewing how to conjugate an irregular verb is a great way for students to reflect on what they are struggling with and have an opportunity to clarify, practice, or strategize with a peer. This normalizes that everyone struggles, and promotes the expectation that extra effort can be the antidote for those struggles.

Make Connections Beyond the Content: This Activator can be easily used to tie your subject into current events. Students can consider which political issues (the economy, the environment, foreign policy, women's issues, education, or immigration) will be deciding factors for them when they eventually get to vote in a presidential election. Participation in this Activator provides young people an opportunity to contemplate how they will participate in and be impacted by our democracy when they are adults.

13

Math

Algebra

1.) The following word problems are all modeled by the equation $y = .5x+3$ if x represents the number of weeks, or $y=2x+3$ if x represents the number of months. Choose one, move to the designated "corner" and solve with a partner:

a.) On January 1st Melissa has $30 and earned $10 a week for delivering groceries to her neighbor. How much money does she have after four months?

b.) Bob collects car magazines. He has three on January 1st and gets two more every month. How many does he have after 16 weeks?

c.) Jamie collects jewelry and is currently obsessed with earrings. She has three pairs and buys a new pair every other week. How many pairs of earrings does she have after 16 weeks?

d.) Alisa collects new iTunes albums. She has three albums and just started working for the Apple store. She is able to save up to buy a new album every two weeks. How many albums does she have after working there for four months?

2.) Look at the functions around the room. Move to one and work with a partner to graph it without a graphing calculator and identify the type of function it is.

a.) $y = \frac{1}{2}x + 4$

b.) $y = -x$

c.) $y = \frac{2}{3}x + 4$

d.) $y = x+3$

e.) $y = 2x - 5$

f.) $y = 7$

g.) $x = -2$

Geometry

Move to a corner that represents one of the geometric solids, and work with a partner to find its volume.

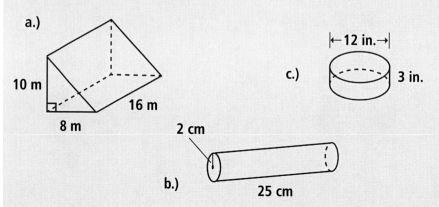

a.)

10 m

16 m

8 m

b.)

2 cm

25 cm

c.)

|← 12 in. →|

3 in.

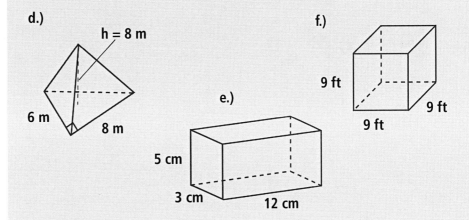

d.)

h = 8 m

6 m

8 m

e.)

5 cm

3 cm

12 cm

f.)

9 ft

9 ft

9 ft

Science

Earth Science

Pretend you are a resident of the country assigned to you. Stand next to one of the following factors that impact the climate in which you live: latitude, large bodies of water, elevation, mountain ranges, vegetation. Turn and talk to a partner about the way this factor affects your climate. (Teacher assigns a country to each student)

Biology

Think about a disease that you might want to research. Stand next to the human body system this disease impacts and talk to a partner about why you're standing there and what you'd like to find out.

Physics

Think about the law of inertia, stand next to the number representing one of the applications and provide an explanation to a partner:

- Blood rushes from your head to your feet while quickly stopping when riding on a descending elevator.
- The head of a hammer can be tightened onto the wooden handle by banging the bottom of the handle against a hard surface.
- A brick is painlessly broken over the hand of a physics teacher by slamming it with a hammer (**CAUTION:** do not attempt this at home!).
- To dislodge ketchup from the bottom of a ketchup bottle, it is often turned upside down and thrust downward at high speeds and then abruptly halted.
- Headrests are placed in cars to prevent whiplash injuries during rear-end collisions.
- While riding a skateboard (or wagon or bicycle), you fly forward off the board when hitting a curb or rock or other object that abruptly halts the motion of the skateboard.

13

Social Studies

Geography

Which of the following do you think has had the greatest influence on your own socialization: family, religion, country, mass media, friends, school, other?

U.S. History

Each of the six images represents life during the roaring twenties. Pick an image/topic to examine up close and then Turn and Talk with a partner/trio to identify three things you can infer from the image about what social changes were taking place during the 1920s. Be prepared to share out with the rest of the class.

(Use images of 1920s: automobiles, women's clothing, household advertisements, movie stars, Prohibition, etc.)

Government

Which political topic would be most important to you when deciding which political candidates to vote for: economy, foreign policy, immigration, women's issues, environment, education, other?

English Language Arts

Writing

Stand next to a number that represents something you accomplished in your second draft of your narrative. Bring your draft and share with your partner what you accomplished.

1.) A beginning that engages and orients the reader by establishing a context and a narrator

2.) Use of dialogue and description to develop characters

3.) Use of description to develop events

4.) Use of sensory details

5.) Transition words that signal shifts from one time frame or setting to another

6.) Satisfying conclusion that follows from and reflects on the narrated events

Reading – Literature

Select a theme from *In the Time of the Butterflies* and talk with a partner about how this theme is developed in the novel. Choose from: courage, family, loyalty, power, religion, or other.

Reading – Informational Text

Stand next to a sign representing one of the four freedoms included in Roosevelt's 1941 State of the Union address. Talk to a partner about Roosevelt's possible reasons for including this freedom in his speech.

- Freedom of speech and expression
- Freedom of every person to worship God in their own way
- Freedom from want
- Freedom from fear

Speaking and Listening

Think of a time when you changed the way you normally speak. Stand next to the sign that represents a reason why you might have adapted your speech in this situation:

- Your relationship with the listener
- Your goal (what you wanted from talking to this person)
- The situation (where and when the conversation took place)
- The listener didn't belong to the same social group (basketball team, chess club, etc.) as you

Language

Stand next to the number that you think best represents the meaning of the word _____ based upon sentence context.

World Languages

Move to the corner that represents what you feel should happen next in the story. Work as a group to craft the details of the ending in (the target) language using vocabulary you have learned over the course of the semester. Example story starter: "*A teenage boy was walking down a city street. 1) He gets a telephone call, 2) Something scary happens, 3) Something funny happens, 4) He is looking for something.*"

Which verb on the upcoming quiz is the most challenging for you to conjugate? Go to that corner and practice conjugating the verb with a partner. Be sure to talk about what makes it so challenging and identify the mistakes you sometimes make.

13

Suggestions for Writing Your Own Four (or more) Corners Activators:

Because this Activator is so flexible, we've seen it work extremely well in all content areas. Whenever your unit includes a list of things/categories/elements/perspectives/etc. you can think about turning it into a Four (or more) Corners. Consider doing a Four (or more) Corners Activator that incorporates interesting images that represent aspects of your unit content. Different images or photographs at each "corner," like the 1920s example referenced earlier is a sure-fire attention grabber and makes for a focused debrief where every student is curious and interested in what the other groups have to say.

YOUR TURN

Design Your Own Four (or more) Corners Activators

A Checklist for Designing Effective Activators:

☐ *Does the prompt support a specific learning outcome?*

☐ *Is the prompt engaging?* Can students respond without feeling anxious or uncomfortable? Do students have enough prior knowledge to feel competent in their responses? Will the prompt ignite curiosity, make content relevant, and challenge students to think at a high level?

☐ *Is the prompt crafted with invitational language that promotes exploration and reduces the need for certainty?* Invitational prompts might begin with "What might...?" "What are some of the...?" or "What is your hunch for why...?"

13

CHAPTER 14

> *Given particular subject matter or a particular concept,*
> *it is easy to ask trivial questions... It is also easy to ask impossibly*
> *difficult questions. The trick is to find the medium questions*
> *that can be answered and that take you somewhere.*
>
> —JEROME BRUNER

Are You More Like

Students get on their feet and compare themselves to key unit concepts.

Since this Activator is "all about me," it creates a big impact on adolescents who are sorting out who they are at school, home, with friends, and in their communities. Are You More Like grabs students' attention by getting them on their feet and asking them to make associations between the content and themselves. The similarities and differences young people discover in this Activator deliver a strong dose of intellectual rigor (Chen, 1999; Cole & McLeod, 1999; Dagher, 1995; Gottfried, 1998; Mason, 1994, 1995). And the novelty and relevance of a task like this helps students store key concepts gained from these comparisons in long-term memory where they can retrieve them for final assessments and beyond.

What are the ways the Are You More Like Activator supports the conditions for engagement?

- Garners **good will** by allowing students to be known and heard by their teacher and peers
- Supports **participation** by offering multiple ways of responding

- Captures **attention** by incorporating movement and providing an audience for students' responses
- Increases **interest** by injecting novelty, surprise, and relevance
- Fosters **effort** by offering review opportunities prior to an assessment

TIME: 10-15 MINUTES

TEACHER PREP LIST

- ❏ Select two terms aligned to learning outcomes in your unit. Make sure **both** of these possess positive or at least neutral qualities, so that the Activator is an opportunity for all students to reflect safely on characteristics or personal assets
- ❏ Identify two spaces that can accommodate half the class
- ❏ Display prompts and student directions
- ❏ Timer

ACTIVATOR SNAPSHOT

STUDENT DIRECTIONS

1. Are you more like _____ or _____ ? Brainstorm a list of words or phrases you associate with each and jot these down in your notebook.

2. Make connections between these words/ phrases and human characteristics and jot these down.

3. Decide whether you are more like _____ or _____ based upon these characteristics and at the signal, move to this side of the room.

4. Talk to a partner about why you're standing where you are.

SET UP THE ACTIVATOR

1. Explain the purpose of the Activator. You might say, *"The Activator we're about to do will give you a chance to reflect on your personal assets or positive qualities and how these connect to key ideas in our unit. And since you'll be on your feet and making connections between course content and yourself, your brain is more likely to pay attention to and remember these important connections."*

2. Review student directions.

3. Tell students they will be asked to compare themselves to one of two things and that you will formulate the question by asking, *"Are you more like...?"*

MODEL AND TEACH

1. Display a different set of terms than the one you will offer students. Do a Think Aloud to brainstorm the positive characteristics of each and to decide which ones describe you best and model moving to that side of the room.

2. Debrief by asking students what they noticed during the Think Aloud.

3. Emphasize that you are asking students which term they are **more like** rather than which one they **like more**.

PRACTICE AND ASSESS

1. Display the prompt and ask students to brainstorm characteristics of the two terms.

2. Provide students with a moment of quiet think time to reflect on which set of characteristics best describes themselves.

3. Invite students to move to the space that represents their response. If some students can't decide and feel they share characteristics of both, explain that they can stand in the middle of the room.

4. Ask students to Turn and Talk with a partner for two minutes about two or three reasons they feel they are more like one term than the other.

5. Circulate to monitor that everyone is paired up and students are engaging in on-task conversations.

6. Let students know when there is one minute remaining.

7. Use a signal to get the group's attention, and ask two or three volunteers from each side of the room to share out some of their reasons for standing in each location.

8. Paraphrase and ask questions to help students elaborate or clarify their responses.

9. Debrief by asking the class a few of the following content and process questions:

Content questions

- What did you hear a peer say that deepened or shifted your thinking about _____ ?
- What is something you learned or realized about _____ ?
- What is something you're wondering about _____ ?

Process questions

- What did you like or dislike about this Activator?
- What did you find challenging?
- If we were to do this Activator again, what might you recommend we do the same or differently?

Thank students for their active participation, affirm understandings and clear up any misconceptions that may have arisen.

TROUBLESHOOTING TIPS

- If your room is too small or you have fixed equipment, consider a secluded hallway to do the Activator.

- It's not uncommon for students to be challenged by thinking symbolically. As a result, it is important to scaffold the thinking process and give students multiple opportunities to practice in order to get good at this college readiness skill. You might consider starting with a Card Sort Activator (see Chapter 9) where students sort sample characteristics for two concepts or terms. Students can then make connections between these characteristics and themselves by using prompts like, *"This reminds me of"* or *"I'm like this when."*

- If a student compares herself or himself to one of the choices in a negative way, try reframing the response. Example: Student: *"I'm like an eraser because I'm always messing things up and have to go back and fix things."* Teacher: *"So you're saying that you're very deliberate in the way you review what you've done and make needed adjustments."*

- If students struggle with listening to one another respectfully during the Activator, incorporate a reflection on Classroom Expectations and Classroom Agreements. Before students try the Activator again, draw the group's attention to the Classroom Expectations and Classroom Agreements and ask them to be mindful of keeping them while engaging in the Activator.

14

VARIATIONS AND EXTENSIONS

- Invite students to shift their position if their classmates' responses have persuaded them to modify their thinking and to explain their reasons for moving.

- Ask students to line up on an imaginary continuum to demonstrate the degree to which they are more like one concept or term or the other.

- Use a Turn and Talk or Popcorn Activator format to respond to an Are You More Like prompt (see Chapter 4 for more on Turn and Talk and Popcorn Activators).
- Ask students to compare themselves to an object in relation to a particular process or course-related task, for example, *"When you solve a geometric proof, are you more like blank or lined paper?"* or *"When you complete a science lab, are you more like a marker or a pencil?"*
- If the Activator is used at the beginning of a lesson, ask students to brainstorm characteristics of two different concepts or terms as part of your Start-of-Class routine.
- Provide prompts and include a brief written reflection after the Activator to help reinforce key concepts: *"I am more like _____ because _____ ."*

Using Are You More Like to Create a High-Performing Community of Learners

For a wonderful source of Are You More Like prompts, we recommend *Are You More Like…?/ What Would It Be Like…?: A Back-to-Back Book of Anytime Questions for Anysize Answers,* by Chris Cavert, Susana Acosta Cavert, and Friends (Wood and Barnes Publishing, 2006).

Asking students to share if they are more like fire or water when it comes to participating in a discussion also provides a forum for reflecting on Habits of Communication. As students explore their style of participating, they can self-reflect on habits that are strengths, like sharing thoughts and ideas, as well as ways they might make some adjustments in order to develop particular habits, like listening respectfully without interrupting. In this way, Are You More Like yields increased self-awareness which creates a High-Performing Community of Learners.

Sample Are You More Like Prompts for Creating a High-Performing Community of Learners

- Are you more like a cookie or a cake?
- When you participate in a discussion, are you more like fire or water?
- When you work in a group, are you more like a cat or a dog?

Using Are You More Like to Support Learning in the Content Areas

Providing Opportunities to Practice Skills and Deepen Understandings: By connecting key characteristics of core academic concepts to themselves, students store the content in long-term memory. For example, a chemistry prompt that asks students to compare themselves to either weight or mass requires them to reflect on the differences between these two concepts and then connect one of these concepts to themselves (Am I consistent? Am I responsive to my environment?). In this way, the likelihood of mass vs. weight sticking in students' minds is far greater than if the teacher simply asked students to explain the differences between these two concepts.

Support Formative Assessment: This Activator provides real-time feedback for learning. As students engage in this exercise, some will start to recognize that they had misconceptions because of what they are hearing their peers say. At the same time, teachers can affirm students' understandings as well as address misunderstandings and provide corrective feedback that will help them make adjustments in their thinking. For example, asking students in a language arts class to consider whether they are more like Hamlet or Laertes allows a teacher to figure out quickly any gaps in students' understandings about the characters, tease out what led to these misconceptions, and help them get back on track with this low-stakes formative assessment.

Inject Relevance Into the Curriculum: The inherent nature of this Activator delivers a big boost of relevance into the middle or high school classroom. Since Are You More Like asks students to compare academic content to themselves, learning outcomes come alive for teenagers whose identities are under construction. Abstract concepts like isolationism and expansionism take on new meaning in a world history class when a teacher invites young people to figure out which term best describes how they define themselves.

14

Math

Algebra

x-y table or x-y axis?

Undefined slope or no slope?

3rd degree or 4th degree function?

Function or relation?

Geometry

Sphere or pyramid?

2-D or 3-D figure?

Regular or irregular polygon?

Concave or convex polygon?

Science

Earth Science

Hydrosphere or lithosphere?

Biology

Bacteria or virus?

Physics

Mass or weight?

Chemistry

Atom or ion?

Social Studies

Geography

Urban or rural?

U.S. History

1950s or 1960s?

World History

Expansionism or isolationism?

Economics

Micro or macro?

Government

Supreme Court or Congress?

English Language Arts

Writing

Feature article or editorial?

Reading – Literature

Hamlet or Laertes?

Reading – Informational Texts

Olive Branch Petition vs. Declaration of Independence?

Speaking and Listening

Dialogue or debate?

Language

Denotation or connotation?

World Languages

In English: verb or an adjective?

In target language: any two key vocabulary words? accent or slang?

14

Suggestions for Writing Your Own Are You More Like Activators:

Look for divergent concepts in your unit that are critical for your students to understand deeply. Tease out whether both have positive or neutral characteristics. After drafting an Are You More Like prompt, test it out on a few colleagues to see what responses it might elicit.

YOUR TURN

Design Your Own Are You More Like Activators

A Checklist for Designing Effective Activators:

☐ *Does the prompt support a specific learning outcome?*

☐ *Is the prompt engaging?* Can students respond without feeling anxious or uncomfortable? Do students have enough prior knowledge to feel competent in their responses? Will the prompt ignite curiosity, make content relevant, and challenge students to think at a high level?

☐ *Is the prompt crafted with invitational language that promotes exploration and reduces the need for certainty?* Invitational prompts might begin with "What might...?" "What are some of the...?" or "What is your hunch for why...?"

CHAPTER

> *Amazingly, the part of the brain that processes movement*
> *is the same part of the brain that processes learning.*
>
> —ERIC JENSEN

Moving Line-Up

Students line up in two lines facing each other and respond to several prompts as they rotate through a series of partners.

Moving Line-Up mixes things up by getting students on their feet and talking to a variety of partners. This highly flexible Activator allows students to clarify, organize, and rehearse their thinking with a peer while providing important practice in active listening. The movement and changing of partners captures students' attention and interest and supports the adolescent brain in holding on to information processed during this Activator.

What are the ways the Moving Line-Up Activator supports the conditions for engagement?

- Fosters **good will** by allowing all students to be known and heard by their peers
- Supports **participation** by offering ways for each student to participate in a low-risk way
- Captures **attention** by incorporating movement
- Increases **interest** by injecting relevance as well as novelty through switching partners
- Encourages **effort** by providing opportunities for practice and feedback
- Supports **investment** by offering ways to establish and reflect on Classroom Expectations and Classroom Agreements

15

TEACHER PREP LIST

- ❏ Design engaging, open-ended prompts aligned with learning outcomes
- ❏ Identify a space where students can line up
- ❏ Identify a student volunteer to model the Activator with you (and if necessary a different prompt)
- ❏ Display prompt and student directions
- ❏ Timer

ACTIVATOR SNAPSHOT

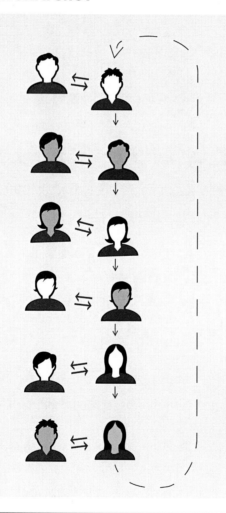

STUDENT DIRECTIONS

1. Line up facing a partner, and think about your response to the prompt.

2. One group ("ones" or "twos") responds for 30 seconds while the other group listens.

3. At the signal, switch roles.

4. The twos move, while the ones stay in position.

5. Repeat with different prompts.

SET UP THE ACTIVATOR

1. Explain the purpose of the Activator. You might say, "*The Activator we're about to do will give you a chance to think out loud and hear what your classmates have*

to say about _____ . *It will also keep your brain alert, since you'll be on your feet and changing partners with each question."*

2. Divide the class in half by counting off: one, two, one, two, etc.

3. Ask the ones to form a line and stand shoulder to shoulder.

4. Ask the twos to line up opposite the ones so that each student has a partner. If there are an uneven number of students, pair two students up who might benefit from having a partner, and ask them to share the talking time.

5. Review student directions.

6. Explain that if a speaker finishes before the 30 seconds have concluded, the listener can ask questions about what the speaker has said.

MODEL AND TEACH

1. Ask for a volunteer who is willing to model a Moving Line-Up conversation with you.

2. Invite the volunteer to position him/herself in the "one" line and put yourself in the "two" line, standing opposite him/her.

3. Provide a sample prompt for the volunteer to respond to while you model listening in engaged silence (making eye contact, nodding head, asking a question if the volunteer finishes speaking before 30 seconds is up).

4. When 30 seconds is up, model responding to the prompt yourself by elaborating on your answer and providing details. When time is up, thank the volunteer by name and explain that since you're a two, you're going to move three spaces to the right while the volunteer stands still. Model moving to the right, giving a high-five or shaking the hand of two people before you stop in front of the third person.

5. Ask students what they noticed about what listening in "engaged silence" and changing partners looked and sounded like as well as what you did when speaking for 30 seconds.

PRACTICE AND ASSESS

1. Say/show the first prompt and give everyone 15 seconds of quiet think time to consider their responses.

2. Ask the ones to begin. Circulate, listen, and support students' active participation and learning.

3. Signal when 30 seconds are over and ask the twos to respond to the same prompt.

4. After this initial round, get some feedback on the amount of time students had to speak. Consider making adjustments in time based upon student feedback.

15

5. Provide feedback on some ways students were interacting effectively and remind them of any behaviors you might want them to practice during the next round. For example, you might say, *"I really like the 'silent' feedback many of you were giving to your partners by making eye contact and nodding your heads. Remember to ask a follow-up question if your partner stops speaking before the time is up."*

6. Ask students to thank their partners by name for sharing and listening, since they will now move to a new partner.

7. Remind students that the twos will move three places to the right while the ones stay where they are. Point out that instead of moving to the right, the student at the end of the twos will move to the beginning of the line. Remind the twos to give high-fives or shake the hands of two people and stop in front of the third student who will be their new partner.

8. Say/display the second prompt. Give everyone 15 seconds of quiet think time to consider their response, and explain that the twos will respond first this time.

9. After both partners have responded, tell the twos to say good-bye to their partners and move three spaces to the right by giving a high-five or shaking the hands of two students before stopping in front of the second. (Varying the number of spaces avoids students anticipating who their partners will be in the next rotation).

10. Explain that the ones will now begin; read the next prompt and repeat step nine with additional prompts.

11. Use a signal to get the group's attention and begin the debrief by asking some of the following content and process questions:

Content questions
- What is one thing you learned or realized about _____ ?
- What are you wondering about _____ ?

Process questions
- What did you like or dislike about this Activator?
- What are some situations when it might be useful to listen first without speaking or interrupting?
- What are some reasons it might be helpful to practice speaking without being interrupted?

Thank students for their active participation, affirm understandings, and clear up any misconceptions that may have emerged.

TROUBLESHOOTING TIPS
- If making a straight line in the classroom is prohibitive, have students line up in a horseshoe or other shape that might be more appropriate for your room. Alternatively, you could use a secluded hallway to do this Activator.

- If students find it challenging to talk and then listen in engaged silence for 30 seconds, begin with a shorter amount of time.

- If students are finishing early and partners are not asking questions, ask a student to help you model asking questions in front of the class. Beforehand, tell this volunteer to respond briefly to the prompt so that you have an opportunity to ask follow-up questions.

- Take an inquiry stance with students and ask them about the value of practicing speaking for an extended amount of time to a partner as well as listening without interrupting. Ask students to think of examples of when this skill might come in handy in school, life, and the future. Remind students that listening attentively is not the same as agreeing with the speaker.

VARIATIONS AND EXTENSIONS

- Ask students to make two concentric circles. The ones form a circle in the middle of the space, standing shoulder to shoulder. They then turn around and face outwards. The twos form a circle around the ones, with each student facing a partner.

- In addition to responding to the prompt, students can paraphrase what they heard their partners say. You will have to do a Think Aloud and provide a model.

- Students can dialogue back and forth in response to a single prompt.

- Ask students to respond to a visual as well as a prompt.

- Change the prompt that the ones and twos respond to. For example, in a math class, you might ask partners to think aloud about two different problems.

- Students can do pre-writing prior to Moving Line-Up, in preparation for talking to their partners.

- Afterwards, students can reflect in writing on how their thinking shifted or deepened as a result of participating in the Activator.

Using Moving Line-Up to Create a High-Performing Community of Learners

15

Moving Line-Up is a great vehicle for building Trust and Belonging. At the beginning of the year, teachers can design prompts that allow students to get to know each other. When young people ask each other a question like, *"What is one thing we wouldn't know about you from just looking at you?"* they can replace assumptions with insights and connections that create a supportive peer cohort essential for learning.

Moving Line-Up can also be used to help students create a classroom vision and lay the groundwork for establishing Classroom Expectations and Classroom Agreements. Talking one-to-one with a peer about what makes a classroom a safe space is a low-risk first step in creating Classroom Agreements that instill ownership and accountability around behaviors that will help everyone work and learn together effectively.

Moving Line-Up Examples for Creating a High-Performing Community of Learners

- What's something we wouldn't know about you from just looking at you?
- What makes a classroom a safe space where you can try your hardest, take risks and make mistakes in order to learn?
- What is one Habit of Learning where you made really big improvements during your small group project? What are some things that helped you make improvements?
- What is one Habit of Learning you would like to focus on during the next group project? What are some things that might help you make improvements with this habit?

Using Moving Line-Up to Support Learning in the Content Areas

Generate Connections to Prior Knowledge: In a language arts classroom, this Activator can bring students immediately into the themes of a book. Prior to reading *Fahrenheit 451*, for example, students might respond to the following prompts: "*What is a book that has had a big impact on you? In what ways did this book impact you? Are there some situations in which books should be banned? Explain your response. What might the following quote by Rabbi Akiba Ben Joseph, about censorship, mean: 'The paper burns, but the words fly away?'*" After participating in this Activator, students have a frame of reference for making sense of what they encounter when they turn to page one. This goes a long way in motivating young people to keep on reading when they encounter a challenging text.

Provide Opportunities to Practice Skills and Deepen Understandings: This Activator offers the multiple hits necessary for learning to occur. For example, the use of Moving Line-Up in a world language class provides students repeated practice telling time in the target language. With each new rotation, students practice pronunciation, use key unit vocabulary, and check for their peer's understanding. In a class of 34 or more students, this individualized practice can help students make progress in the targeted language more quickly.

Offer Opportunities for Formative Assessment. As teachers listen in on students' conversations during a Moving Line-Up, they gather critical information about what their students know and can do. An algebra teacher who circulates up and down the lines while students are discussing with partners which solution is correct and which is an error, can determine patterns of understanding, uncover misconceptions and notice which students might be challenged to respond at any length. As a result, they are able to provide immediate feedback following the Activator and adjust or differentiate the rest of today's or tomorrow's lesson to meet the needs of their students.

Prepare Students for Assessments: This Activator makes review and revision interactive and engaging for adolescents. For example, earth science students can participate in a Moving Line-Up Activator prior to a unit exam on erosion, by responding to the following prompts: "*What are some ways human activity has altered the surface of the earth? What are different types of erosion? What are some problems caused by erosion? What are some ways of solving erosion problems?*" Talking to peers in this low-risk way about these questions helps students actively study by retrieving what they have learned and assessing their responses in light of their partners' answers. It also provides one more opportunity for teachers to offer feedback to students that can help them be successful on the exam.

Inject Relevance into the Curriculum. The multiple one-to-one conversations during this Activator build a bridge between the content and the real world. In a world history class, Moving Line-Up can be used to help students make important connections by discussing a question like, "*How is the industrialization of countries around the world today impacting the United States?*" In this way, students understand the value of what they encounter in the classroom and are more likely to hold on to what they are learning.

15

Math

Algebra

Pairing #1:

Which is the correct solution? Which is the error? Explain your response to your partner.

What do you get when you square 4x?

Solution A:

$(4x)^2$

$(4)^2 (x)^2$

$16x^2$

Solution B:

$4x^2$

Pairing #2:

Which is the correct solution? Which is the error? Explain your response to your partner.

Simplify $(-3)^2$

Solution A:

-3^2

$-(3)(3)$

-9

Solution B:

$(-3)^2$

$(-3)(-3)$

9

Pairing #3

Which is the correct solution? Which is the error? Explain your response to your partner.

Subtract $4x - 5$ from $x^2 + 3x - 5$

Solution A:

$x^2 + 3x - 5 - 4x - 5$

$x^2 - x - 10$

Solution B:

$x^2 + 3x - 5 - (4x - 5)$

$x^2 + 3x - 5 - 4x + 5$

$x^2 - x$

Geometry

Pairing #1:

Which is the correct solution? Which is the error? Explain your response to your partner.

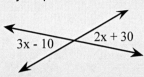

Solution A:

$$3x - 10 = -2x + 30$$
$$ +2x \quad +2x$$
$$3x - 8 = 30$$
$$ +8 \quad +8$$
$$3x = 38$$
$$3 \quad 3$$
$$x = 38/3$$

Solution B:

$$3x - 10 = 2x + 30$$
$$ -2x \quad -2x$$
$$3x - 12 = 30$$
$$ +12 \quad +12$$
$$3x = 42$$
$$3 \quad 3$$
$$x = 14$$

Pairing #2:

Which is the correct solution? Which is the error? Explain your response to your partner.

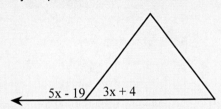

Solution A:

$$5x - 19 = 3x + 4$$
$$ -3x \quad -3x$$
$$2x - 19 = 4$$
$$ +19 \quad +19$$
$$2x = 23$$
$$2 \quad 2$$
$$x = 23/2$$

Solution B:

$$5x - 19 + 3x + 4 = 180$$
$$8x - 15 = 180$$
$$ +15 \quad +15$$
$$8x = 195$$
$$8 \quad 8$$
$$x = 195/8$$

Pairing #3:

Which is the correct solution? Which is the error? Explain your response to your partner.

In the figure at right, m∠1 is 48°. What is the m∠2? Explain your reasoning.

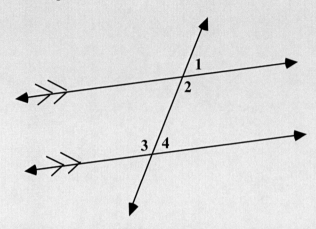

Solution A: m∠2 is 48° because ∠1 and ∠2 are vertical angles.

Solution B: m∠2 is 132° because ∠1 and ∠2 are supplementary angles.

Science

Earth Science

Pairing #1: What are some of the ways human activities have altered the surface of the earth?

Pairing #2: What are different types of erosion?

Pairing #3: What are some problems caused by erosion?

Pairing #4: What are some ways of solving erosion problems?

Biology

Pairing #1: What are some things that a plant and an animal cell have in common?

Pairing #2: What are some differences between a plant and an animal cell?

Pairing #3: Show pictures of plant and animal cells and discuss: Is this a plant or animal cell?

Chemistry

What are the similarities and differences between these type of reactions:

Pairing #1: Synthesis and decomposition?

Pairing #2: Single replacement and double replacement?

Pairing #3: Combustion and acid-base?

Physics

Pairing #1: A ball is rolling across the top of a billiard table and slowly rolls to a stop. Why?

Pairing #2: Your friend says that inertia is a force that keeps things in their place, either at rest or in motion. Do you agree? Why or why not?

Pairing #3: Why do you lurch forward in a bus that suddenly slows? Why do you lurch backward when it speeds up? What law applies here?

Social Studies

Geography

Pairing #1: What is one climate in which you would like to live or vacation and why?

Pairing #2: What is one climate in which would you not want to live? Why?

Pairing #3: What are three ways that the climate in which we live differs from a tropical climate?

U.S. History

Project political cartoons from the Progressive Era for each pairing, and have partners work together to determine the artist's message (Alternatively, create and distribute a handout with three to four political cartoons numbered for each pair to analyze.)

World History

In what ways did Europe's industrialization impact…

Pairing #1: Family Life?

Pairing #2: Economic?

Pairing #3: Women?

Pairing #4: Children?

Pairing #5: Non-industrialized countries/regions?

15

Economics

Apply the definition of scarcity to answer the following questions:

Pairing #1: Is sand scarce?

Pairing #2: Are pencils scarce?

Pairing #3: Is water scarce?

U.S. Government

Distinguish between National, State, and Local government powers: Who has the power to...

Pairing #1: Make laws?

Pairing #2: Regulate commerce?

Pairing #3: Determine the driving age?

English Language Arts

Writing

Pairing #1: What is your editorial's claim and what are two pieces of supporting evidence?

Pairing #2: What is your editorial's claim and what are two counterclaims to yours?

Pairing #3: What is your editorial's claim? What is one counterclaim? Name a strength and a limit to this counterclaim.

Reading – Literature

Prior to reading *Fahrenheit 451*:

Pairing #1: What is a book that has had a big impact on you? In what ways did this book impact you?

Pairing #2: Are there some situations in which books should be banned? Explain your response.

Pairing #3: What are some things Rabbi Akiba Ben Joseph might mean by saying about censorship: "The paper burns, but the words fly away?"

Reading – Informational Texts

After reading the *New York Times* article, "On Road to Recovery, Past Adversity Provides a Map" (January 3, 2011):

Pairing #1: What are some factors that can impact a person's resilience, according to the article?

Pairing #2: According to the article, what are some things people can learn from experiencing negative events?

Pairing #3: What connections can you make between what you read in the article and your own life?

Speaking and Listening

Pairing #1: What are some ways you might describe the speaker's point of view?

Pairing #2: What supporting evidence did the speaker offer to support their point of view?

Pairing #3: What might be examples of distorted or exaggerated evidence that the speaker used?

Language

After reading Judith Ortiz Cofer's poem "The Latin Deli: An Ars Poetica,"

Pairing #1: What are some things the speaker might want to communicate about The Patroness of Exiles by saying she "spends her days...selling canned memories?" What figure of speech is used?

Pairing #2: What are some things the speaker might want to communicate about the old man's items that "he reads to her like poetry?" What figure of speech is used?

Pairing #3: What are some things the speaker might want to communicate by describing some of the deli customers' hearts as "closed ports that she must trade with?" What figure of speech is used here?

World Languages

In target language:

General Greetings

Pairing #1: Hi my name is _____ . What is your name?

Pairing #2: Nice to meet you. Nice to meet you, too.

Pairing #3: Hello, how are you? I am great/well/okay/so-so/tired/bad/ other appropriate response.

Telling Time

Excuse me, do you know the time? (teacher changes manual clock for each rotation)

Telephone Conversations for any theme

Practice scripted dialogue (telephone conversation related to unit topic/ theme)

Suggestions for Writing Your Own Moving Line-Up Activators:

Consider prompts aligned with learning outcomes that would elicit multiple responses so that each partner has an opportunity to respond in different ways. To merit investing time in this Activator, we recommend designing at least three different questions. When crafting these, you might want to keep Bloom's taxonomy in mind and begin by asking questions that require basic understanding before moving into more complex ones that ask students to apply, analyze, evaluate, and create.

YOUR TURN

Design Your Own Moving Line-Up Activators

15

CHAPTER 16

> *Since our "thinking cap" is strongly influenced by patterns,*
> *not facts, remembering information is maximized*
> *when it is provided in contextual, event-oriented situations*
> *which include...location changes [and]...novelty.*
>
> —Eric Jensen

Rotation Stations

Students move around in small groups to different stations where they work together responding to prompts or completing tasks.

Adolescents respond enthusiastically to novelty and movement, which stimulate the brain's attentive focus (Hannaford, 2005 and University College, London, 2006). Rotation Stations novelty and movement also provides multiple, varied exposures to a topic or skill and strengthens the brain's capacity to encode what it encounters. As students travel around, processing and practicing with a small group of peers, their understanding and skills sharpen with each rotation. While this Activator requires more teacher preparation than others, it offers a big payoff in student engagement.

What are the ways the Rotation Station Activator supports the conditions for engagement?

- Garners **good will** by filling the room with students' voices
- Supports **participation** by structuring small group conversations and offering a way to build on the thinking of others
- Captures **attention** by incorporating movement and making students' thinking visible to their peers
- Increases **interest** by injecting novelty through changing stations at regular intervals

- Supports **effort** by providing multiple and varied opportunities for practicing skills and rehearsing ideas in small groups
- Fosters **investment** by collecting students' thinking around Classroom Expectations and Classroom Agreements.

TIME: 20-45 MINUTES (depending upon the complexity of tasks at each station)

TEACHER PREP LIST

- ❏ Develop engaging station prompts or tasks aligned with learning outcomes that students can work together on without teacher assistance and that require approximately the same amount of time to complete. Have an additional, compelling prompt or artifact for groups that finish early

- ❏ Set up station materials and display instructions around the room

- ❏ Decide how you will group students

- ❏ Display student sentence starters

- ❏ Timer

- ❏ Graphic organizer (optional)

- ❏ Chart paper and different colored markers (optional)

ACTIVATOR SNAPSHOT

STUDENT DIRECTIONS

1. At the signal, move to your assigned station.

2. Work with your group to respond to the prompt or complete the task.

3. Jot down your group's response on a graphic organizer, notebook or chart paper.

4. At the signal, move to the next station and repeat.

16

SET UP THE ACTIVATOR

1. Explain the purpose of the Activator. You might say, "*This Activator will get you moving around the room to different stations in order to explore/practice _____ . Moving around every _____ minutes and talking with your group about what you find at each station will keep your brains alert and help you remember what you're learning.*"

2. Review student directions. Tell students how much time they will have at each station. (Two to ten minutes at each station, depending upon the number of stations and the complexity of the tasks.)

3. Draw students' attention to the different stations by reading the sign or prompt at each one and explaining the tasks, as needed.

4. Divide students up into groups of three or four and distribute graphic organizers or markers as needed.

MODEL AND TEACH

1. Emphasize that students are expected to interact with their group members to process the question or material at each station. You might provide some sentence starters to support these conversations, for example: "*What does everyone think about _____ ? I'm wondering if we want to _____ . I agree/disagree with the idea _____ because _____ .*"

2. If students are using graphic organizers, clarify if all group members are expected to write the same thing. If so, you might provide some sentence starters to help students synthesize their ideas, for example: "*So we're saying _____ . It sounds like we agree that _____ . What will we all write down?*"

3. If students are recording responses on chart paper at each station, explain that each group will use the same colored marker at all stations and will add their responses to what the previous group(s) recorded. If they have a question about a response, encourage them to put a question mark next to it on the chart paper. You might provide sentence starters to support these conversations, for example: "*What are some additional ideas about _____ ? Do we all agree that _____ ? Is there anything here we have a question about?*" Encourage group members to take turns recording what the group says.

4. If students will sit at each station, model how to pick up their chairs/desks and move to the initial station.

PRACTICE AND ASSESS

1. Assign each group to a station and instruct them to move there and begin.

2. Circulate, listen, and support students' active participation and learning.

3. Use a timer to keep students on track with how many minutes they spend at each station.

4. If students have not yet written down anything, prompt them to make sure they complete writing within the next minute. Check in to see if groups need more time and make any needed adjustments.

5. Use a signal to get the group's attention. Offer feedback about ways students were interacting effectively. For example, *"Thank you for working together to make sure you and your group members all wrote the same thing on your graphic organizer."* Remind students of any behaviors you want them to practice when they get to the next station, for example, *"When you get to the next station, I encourage you to ask each other what you think about the question."*

6. If students are brainstorming responses on chart paper, remind them to add to what previous groups have written as well as to use question marks if there is a comment they are wondering about.

7. Continue until students have rotated through all the stations. If students are charting their responses for others to see, you might need to increase time with each rotation since they will need to think a little longer about what to add to the previously recorded responses.

8. Use a signal to get the group's attention and begin the debrief by asking some of the following content and process questions:

Content questions
- What is one thing you learned about _____ as a result of this Activator?
- What station helped you the most with reaching today's learning outcome? In what way?
- What is one station that raised a question for you regarding _____ ?

Process Questions
- What was it like to participate in this Rotation Stations Activator?
- Which station was most challenging? What are some reasons it was challenging?
- If we were to do this Activator again, are there some stations you might want to add?

Thank students for their active participation, affirm understandings, and clear up any misconceptions that might have emerged.

NOTE: If groups recorded their responses at each station you might debrief Rotation Stations with a Post It Up Activator (Chapter 6). Provide each student with stickers, sticky notes, or a marker, and ask them to read all of the pieces of chart paper and "vote" for three to five responses they feel are most important to pay attention to. Consider using generic questions or generate your own more specific ones: *"What do you see or notice? So what do you think it means or why does it matter? Now what should we be asking, doing, or trying to understand?"*

16

TROUBLESHOOTING TIPS

- If your class is large, make two sets of stations or have two groups of three students working at each station.

- If students need support in working collaboratively, have students take on roles in their groups (see some suggested group roles below). If students need more support working together, consider providing one graphic organizer to the group (this will require you to make photocopies for each student afterwards). Limiting the resources in this way encourages students to be more dependent on one another.

Some Suggested Group Roles:

Facilitator: Gets group started, initiates group discussion, monitors work progress, ensuring that everyone listens and speaks respectfully

Timekeeper: Keeps an eye on the clock and periodically reminds group or remaining time.

Clarifier: Checks with teacher to clarify rules, guidelines and instructions when the group has questions.

Resource Manager: Picks up, distributes, collects and puts away materials.

For more group roles and descriptions, refer to Carol Miller Lieber's *Making Learning Real: Reaching and Engaging All Learners in Secondary Classrooms*, pp. 280-281 (Educators for Social Responsibility, 2009).

VARIATIONS AND EXTENSIONS

- If moving around in your room is just not possible, have students stay seated and rotate materials instead. Each group will receive one set of materials, and when the first task is completed and time is called, a person in each group passes materials to the next one in a clockwise fashion. Repeat until the materials have rotated through all the groups.

- If you are using a Rotation Stations Activator to expose students to new content, you might follow up with a Quick Jot and Turn and Talk Activator (Chapter 4), so students can synthesize their thinking about what they encountered at each station.

- Create one or two "open" stations that groups can move to if they finish early.

- Once a group has completed a task they can become helpers for another group. If a group is stuck, they can request to ask a question from one of these helpers. This builds a High-Performing Community of Learners by encouraging students to rely on each other, not just on you, for assistance.

Using Rotation Stations to Create a High-Performing Community of Learners

Rotation Stations is a great tool for unpacking Habits of Learning. Posting key habits on separate pieces of chart paper where students brainstorm with their classmates exactly what it looks like and sounds like to demonstrate each one will set them up for success. When young people have the opportunity to take an abstract Habit of Participation/Communication like, "*I used positive, nonaggressive language to express myself, ask for help, and get what I need,*" and make it as concrete as possible, they have clear learning targets and can self-assess more effectively.

In our own classrooms, we have witnessed how this Activator is a powerful starting place building a Classroom Agreement around respect, a concept that has widely different meanings to different people. Rotation Station questions like, "*What are some things students do and say that show respect to other students?*" and "*What are some things students do and say that show disrespect to other students?*" invite young people to slow down and get on the same page with concrete descriptors. By including questions like, "*What are some things teachers do and say that show respect to students?*" and "*What are some things teachers do and say that show disrespect to students?*" teachers demonstrate their commitment to creating a safe learning environment, signal their shared accountability, and obtain valuable information for working effectively with groups of students throughout the year.

Rotation Station Examples for Creating a High-Performing Community of Learners

Habits of Learning T-Charts

Brainstorm what each Habit of Learning might look like and sound like at each station. Examples:

- **Habit of Communication:** I use positive, nonaggressive language to express myself, ask for help, and get what I need.
- **Habit of Work:** I follow directions and ask questions when I don't understand.
- **Habit of Self-Discipline:** I handle mistakes, setbacks, stress, and frustration effectively.
- **Habit of Mind:** I'm curious and I ask questions to probe for deeper understanding.
- **Habit of Participation:** I work cooperatively with others and do my fair share of work.

Classroom Expectations/Agreements Charts

- Brainstorm examples of what each Classroom Expectation or Classroom Agreement might look like and sound like at each station.

16

Respect Rotation Stations Brainstorm

Student-to-Student Respect
What are some things students do and say that show **respect** towards other students?

Student-to-Student Disrespect
What are some things students do and say that show **disrespect** towards other students?

Teacher-to-Student Respect
What are some things teachers do and say that show **respect** towards students?

Teacher-to-Student Disrespect
What are some things teachers do and say that show **disrespect** towards students?

Student-to-Teacher Respect
What are some things students do and say that show **respect** towards teachers?

Student-to-Teacher Disrespect
What are some things students do and say that show **disrespect** towards teachers?
What are some ways students can disagree with a teacher and show respect at the same time?
What are some ways teachers can correct and discipline students and show respect at the same time?

Using Rotation Stations to Support Learning in the Content Areas

Generate Connections to Prior Knowledge: Rotation Stations can function like mini-museum galleries, where students encounter artifacts that will help them step into new content. In a U.S. history class, students might move around the room and discuss their observations and inferences about photographs depicting aspects of World War I warfare, such as life in the trenches, the first machine guns, maps of stagnant battle lines, the first tanks, the first gas masks and ailments and medical treatments. This Activator provides students with vivid images they can connect to textbook descriptions they will read about afterwards. And with the Internet warehousing so many historical images, finding compelling visuals is relatively easy. Putting color printouts in sheet protectors helps preserve them from year to year.

Provide Opportunities to Practice Skills and Deepen Understanding: In a science classroom, Rotation Stations catches students' attention by putting a lab on its feet. As part of a physics unit on friction, students can move around the room, testing out hypotheses about the impact different surfaces have on friction when force is exerted on a wooden block. Although students might just as easily conduct all six experiments while seated at one table, isolating each one to a different station and requiring students to move sharpens the brain's attentive focus on the experiments and ramps up curiosity (What are we going to find at the next station?). The increased understanding that results makes the additional setup this Activator requires on the teacher's part well worth it.

Support Formative Assessment: The highly interactive nature of Rotation Stations allows students to obtain real-time feedback from peers and offers on-the-spot information to teachers about what students know and can do in a world languages class. This Activator provides all students with multiple practice opportunities in the target language as they introduce themselves, greet one another, offer where they are from, provide directions, have a mock telephone conversation, and tell time. Through repeated practice and listening to peers, as well as reflection during the debrief, students realize what rolls off the tongue and what they might need to focus on further. At the same time, the teacher circulates and collects data that will inform her next steps with the class as well as with individual students.

Prepare Students for a Final Assessment: This Activator is an interactive way to make preparation for a final assessment engaging. In a biology unit on the circulatory system, students might prepare for an upcoming exam by listing what they know about key terms, including heart, lungs, veins, arteries, exchange of gases, and capillaries. Working in these informal, interactive "study groups" helps students encode the information in long-term memory.

Inject Relevance Into the Curriculum: Rotation Stations can connect students to content in order to develop skills and hold onto new information more easily. In an English language arts class, students might engage in this Activator as a way to practice developing claims and counterclaims around issues that matter to them. Rehearsing in small groups with teen-centered claims like, *"Parents should let teens make their own decisions"* helps adolescents focus on skill building without getting weighed down by content. When talking with peers about topics that have an emotional charge, students' motivation increases and they have the opportunity to practice balancing feelings with sound reasoning in their writing.

16

Math

Algebra
Logarithms Review

Station #1

1.) The cost of a television set has increased by two percent each year. In 1999, the average television cost $400. Write an exponential model to represent this data.

2.) Using your model, calculate how much a TV will cost in 2014.

3.) Using your model, calculate the approximate year when a TV will cost $500.

Station #2

Simplify without using a calculator.

1.) $\log_{1/3} 81$

2.) $\log_5 (1/25)$

3.) $\log 1000$

4.) $\ln e^{-5}$

5.) $(e^4)(e^{-7})(e^{2x})$

Station #3

1.) Expand $\ln 9x^2 y^3$

2.) Condense $2 \log_3 5 + \log_3 x - 4 \log_3 y$

3.) Expand $\log \dfrac{10y^3}{3x^2}$

4.) Condense $(4 \log_7 x + \log_7 y) - (\frac{1}{2} \log_7 x + 3 \log_7 y)$

Station #4

Solve for x.

1.) $4^{x-5} = 32^{x+1}$

2.) $e^{2x} - 2 = 5$

3.) $3 \log_4 (x - 5) = 9$

4.) $5 - \ln 2x = 1$

Station #5

1.) $\log_{81} 3$

2.) $\sqrt[3]{8e^{9x}}$

3.) $\log_{3/4} \dfrac{16}{9}$

4.) $e^{\ln 4x}$

5.) $\dfrac{5e^6}{10e^{2x}}$

Station #6

1.) Expand $\qquad \log_7 (14x^2y)^3$

2.) Condense $\qquad 3(\log_3 x + \log_3 2) - \log_3 x$

3.) Expand $\qquad \log_3 \dfrac{(2y)^3}{x^2}$

4.) Condense $\qquad (2\log_7 x - \log_7 y) + (\log_7 x - 4\log_7 y)$

Station #7

1.) You purchased a car for $15,000. Your car depreciates at a rate of 11% each year. Write an exponential model to represent this data.

2.) Using your model, calculate how much your car will cost in 5 years.

3.) Using your model, calculate how old your car will be when it costs $2,611.

Station #8

Solve for x.

1.) $\log_4 (x + 5) = \log_4 (9x - 3)$

2.) $e^{2x} = e^{15}$

3.) $3^{x-2} = 5$

4.) $\ln x^2 = 3$

Geometry
Compositions of Transformations

Station #1

Given $\triangle TRY$ with vertices T(−2, 3), R(3, 6), Y(1, −1)

   a.) Perform the composition of transformations $r_{x-axis} \circ R_{90°}$

   b.) State the single transformation equivalent to the above composition of transformations

16

Station #2

Given △CAT with vertices C(–5, 3), A(2, 6), T(7, 1)

    a.) Perform the composition of transformations $R_{90°} \circ r_{y=x}$

    b.) State the single transformation equivalent to the above composition of transformations

Station #3

Given △DOG with vertices D(1, 2), O(5, 7), G(8, 4)

    a.) Perform the composition of transformations $r_{x-axis} \circ r_{y=x}$

    b.) State the single transformation equivalent to the above composition of transformations

Station #4

Given △ELF with vertices E(1, –5), L(6, –4), F(3, –1)

    a.) Perform the composition of transformations $R_{180°} \circ R_{270°}$

    b.) State the single transformation equivalent to the above composition of transformations

Science

Earth Science

Topographic Map Skill Stations

Station #1: Interpret contour lines to determine elevation

Station #2: Identify water features

Station #3: Use latitude and longitude to determine location

Station #4: Identify a correct profile

Station #5: Use scale to calculate distance

Station #6: Interpret contour lines to determine direction a river flows

Biology

Circulatory Systems Brainstorm

At each station jot down everything you know about the term on the chart paper, adding to the thinking of the previous groups as well as recording questions.

Station #1: Heart

Station #2: Lungs

Station #3: Capillaries

Station #4: Blood

Station #5: Arteries

Station #6: Veins

Station #7: Exchange of Gases

Chemistry

Catch a Mole Stations.

Calculate the mass of moles for the chemical at each station.

Station #1: Copper Metal

Calculate:

1.) The mass of 1 mole
2.) 0.6 moles
3.) 9.03×10^{-23} atoms

Station #2: Zinc Metal

Calculate:

1.) Half of one mole
2.) 0.24 moles
3.) 6.02×10^{22} atoms

Station #3: Sodium Chloride

Calculate:

1.) 0.91 of one mole
2.) 8.56×10^{-1} mole
3.) 1.05×10^{23} atoms

Station #4: Magnesium Sulfate Heptahydrate

Calculate:

1.) 0.14 mole
2.) Mass of 0.16 mole
3.) Mass of 7.44×10^{21} atoms

Station #5: Sodium hydrogen carbonate

Calculate:

1.) Mass of .05 mole
2.) Mass of 1.08 moles
3.) 3.7×10^{22} atoms

Physics
Surface Tension and Friction Stations

At each station are three books, a wooden surface and a spring scale. There is a block with a different surface at each station. Make a hypothesis about the effect of the surface on the amount of friction, place the books on the block, pull on the scale, and record the maximum force needed before it moves as well as the force needed to keep it moving.

16

Station #1: Bare wood block

Station #2: Block with sandpaper surface

Station #3: Block with foam rubber surface

Station #4: Block with wax paper surface

Station #5: Block with carpeted surface

Station #6: Block with oily surface

Social Studies

Geography

Atlas Skill-Builder focusing on target region or country

Station #1: Find and label the identified political features on your map

Station #2: Find and label the identified physical features on your map

Station #3: Practice with latitude and longitude: find the following locations and mark them on your map

Station #4: Create a key and draw symbols on your map to show the top five economic activities in the region

Station #5: Create a key and draw symbols on your map to show the top three languages spoken in the region

Station #6: Create a key and draw symbols on your map to show the religions represented in the region

U.S. History

Discuss and jot down at least three observations for each photograph in the left column, and one question and one inference about warfare conditions during World War I in the right column. At each station are one to two historical photographs or images representing:

Station #1: Trench warfare

Station #2: First machine guns

Station #3: Map of stagnant battle lines

Station #4: First tanks

Station #5: First gas masks and chemical weapons

Station #6: Ailments and medical treatment

World History

Review the information card at each station and annotate your timeline of key events connected to the Russian Revolution and the birth of the Soviet Union with a brief description and an illustration.

Materials: blank timeline from 1914–1923 and short summaries of the following:

Station #1: Russian industrialization and social and economic conditions

Station #2: World War I

Station #3: Tsar Nicholas

Station #4: February Revolution

Station #5: October Revolution

Station #6: Russian Civil War

English Language Arts

Writing

Brainstorm relevant evidence to develop the claim as well as counterclaims at each station.

Station #1: Schools should offer fast food options like McDonalds and Taco Bell.

Station #2: Parents should let teens make their own decisions.

Station #3: Students should be able to select what courses they take in high school.

Station #4: Students should be able to listen to MP3 players on headphones during independent activities in class.

Station #5: High school should start at 10 a.m.

Station #6: Sex education should be increased in schools.

Reading – Literature

Discuss and respond to the artifacts at each station connected to *Grapes of Wrath* that will help you generate prior knowledge about the novel's setting and themes.

Station #1: Dorothea Lange's *Migrant Mother* photograph. Make observations and draw inferences about where the woman is, what she is thinking/feeling, what just happened, and what she might do next.

Station #2: Woody Guthrie's *Dustbowl Refugee*. Read the lyrics and listen to the song, and make inferences about the speaker: *Who is he? Why is he a refugee? What happened?*

Station #3: Discuss and take notes on the following question: *What are some things that keep a family together?*

Station #4: Read the following quote from *Grapes of Wrath* and make inferences about who "us people" might be and who "them people" might refer to in the novel:

"Why, Tom - us people will go on livin' when all them people is gone. Why, Tom, we're the people that live. They ain't gonna wipe us out. Why, we're the people. We go on."

"We take a beatin' all the time."

"I know." Ma chuckled."Maybe that makes us tough. Rich fellas come up an' they die, an' their kids ain't no good, an' they die out. But, Tom, we keep a-comin'. Don' you fret none, Tom. A different time's comin."

Station #5: Map of Dustbowl migration routes. Make observations and inferences about causes behind the Dustbowl migration patterns as well as impact on migrants.

Station #6: Cover and title station. Make observations and inferences about the illustration on the book's cover and the metaphorical meaning of the novel's title.

Reading – Informational Texts

Process the feature article you read about _____ by completing the task at each station as a group:

Station #1: Points of View Station: Identify different points of view in the article.

Station #2: Important Facts Station: List three important facts found in the article and draw a symbol for each.

Station #3: Look Who's Talking Station: Make inferences about what people might be saying in the accompanying photograph and put these in speech bubbles.

Station #4: Alternate Title Station: Develop an alternate title in seven words or less that captures a key idea in the article.

Station #5: Discussion Station: Discuss and take notes on a teacher-generated inferential question connected to the article.

Station #6: Craft Station: Use context to determine meaning or connotation of a teacher-identified key word in the article.

Speaking and Listening

Logical Fallacy Stations. Review definitions and examples of logical fallacies and post your own examples on chart paper.

Station #1: Ad Hominem - Attacking the individual instead of the argument. Example: You are so stupid your argument couldn't possibly be true. Example: I figured that you couldn't possibly get it right, so I ignored your comment.

Station #2: Cause and Effect - Assuming that the effect is related to a cause because the events occur together.

Example: When the rooster crows, the sun rises. Therefore, the rooster causes the sun to rise.

Example: When the fuel light goes on in my car, I soon run out of gas. Therefore, the fuel light causes my car to run out of gas.

Station #3: Fallacy of Division - Assuming that what is true of the whole is true for the parts.

Example: That car is blue. Therefore, its engine is blue.

Example: Your family is weird. That means that you are weird too.

Station #4: Poisoning the Well - Presenting negative information about a person before he/she speaks so as to discredit the person's argument.

Example: Frank is pompous, arrogant, and thinks he knows everything. So, let's hear what Frank has to say about the subject.

Example: Don't listen to him because he is a loser.

Station #5: Red Herring - Introducing a topic not related to the subject at hand.

Example: I know your car isn't working right. But, if you had gone to the store one day earlier, you'd not be having problems.

Example: I know I forgot to deposit the check into the bank yesterday. But nothing I do pleases you.

Station #6: Begging the Question - Assuming the thing to be true that you are trying to prove. It is circular.

Example: God exists because the Bible says so. The Bible is inspired. Therefore, we know that God exists.

Example: I am a good worker because Frank says so. How can we trust Frank? Simple: I will vouch for him.

Language

Conventions Editing Stations

Edit the anonymous student examples of convention errors found at each station (two sets of stations are used to accommodate class size):

Stations #1 and 4: Passive to active voice

Stations #2 and 5: Sentence combining

Stations #3 and 6: Spelling: Their/there/they're

16

World Languages

Target Language Skill Builder for any unit with a central theme:

Station #1: Vocabulary-Nouns: Using vocabulary flashcards, quiz each other in your group.

Station #2: Constructing Sentences: Using the word bank, write three correct sentences in the target language.

Station #3: Culture: Explore the culture pictures and then think of and write down in your notebook (in English) one question, one observation, and one way one of the pictures connects to something you already know about the culture of (target language country/region).

Station #4: Grammar: Find the errors in the sample sentences, then write the sentences correctly in your notebook.

Station #5: Pronunciation: Practice the dialogue with a partner; in your notebook write down any words that you don't know the meaning of and any words that are challenging to pronounce.

Station #6: Vocabulary-Verbs: Write down each of the verbs in your notebook and draw a symbol or image to represent each meaning.

Target Language Speaking Practice: At each station, read the written dialogue aloud with a partner, inserting appropriate vocabulary when it indicates to do so.

Station #1: Introductions dialogue (My name is _____ . What is your name?).

Station #2: Greeting dialogue (Hello, How are you? I am _____ .).

Station #3: Where are you from? dialogue.

Station #4: Directions dialogue (Where is the _____ ?).

Station #5: Mock Telephone call dialogue.

Station #6: Time dialogue (What time is it? What time do you go sleep?).

Suggestions for Writing Your Own Rotation Stations Activators:

This is a great Activator to use if you teach a complex topic that requires students to build a lot of background knowledge. If you use a PowerPoint presentation with a lot of slides/visuals to teach background knowledge, consider turning part of it into a Rotation Stations Activator. If you teach a skill that you know students will need significant practice to master, create a Rotation Station Activator to support this practice and get ready to witness the benefits of injecting novelty, collaborative interaction, and physical movement into skills practice.

YOUR TURN

Design Your Own Rotation Stations Activators

A Checklist for Designing Effective Activators:

☐ *Does the prompt support a specific learning outcome?*

☐ *Is the prompt engaging?* Can students respond without feeling anxious or uncomfortable? Do students have enough prior knowledge to feel competent in their responses? Will the prompt ignite curiosity, make content relevant, and challenge students to think at a high level?

☐ *Is the prompt crafted with invitational language that promotes exploration and reduces the need for certainty?* Invitational prompts might begin with "What might...?" "What are some of the...?" or "What is your hunch for why...?"

16

---

*If brain-based pedagogy could be summed up in one sentence,
it would be, knowledge should be socially created.*

—MICHAEL SLAVKIN

Mix and Mingle

Students respond to prompts or share information with a series of partners as they move around the room.

This Activator builds a class cohort by setting the expectation that students will interact with different classmates on a regular basis and everyone's ideas and voice are valued. Mix and Mingle can move students from a comfort zone of exchanging of ideas with just one or two peers into a growth zone of conversing with several different partners. As students talk with a variety of peers, they gain important practice in sharing their thinking and valuing other perspectives, which enhances their capacity for engaging in meaningful social interactions in school, careers, and life.

NOTE: *We positioned this Activator last, since it has a number of moving parts. While making your way through the directions, if you find it a little challenging to imagine what the Activator might look like, consider scanning the content area examples that follow to firm up your understanding.*

What are the ways the Mix and Mingle Activator supports the conditions for engagement?

- Garners **good will** by respecting students' individual perspectives and expertise
- Supports **participation** by creating connectedness through partnering with other students
- Captures **attention** by incorporating movement and frequent rotations

- Increases **interest** by injecting novelty and relevance
- Fosters **effort** by rehearsing thinking with a series of partners
- Supports **investment** when used as a vehicle to reflect on Classroom Expectations and Classroom Agreements

TIME: 10-15 MINUTES

TEACHER PREP LIST

- ❏ Design three to seven engaging prompts (questions, quotes or images) aligned with a learning outcome

- ❏ Print prompts on different colored slips of paper or clearly number each slip of paper on the back (to help students see which prompt a classmate has)

- ❏ Pens/pencils

- ❏ Display student directions

- ❏ Create and make copies of graphic organizers (optional)

- ❏ Timer

ACTIVATOR SNAPSHOT

STUDENT DIRECTIONS

1. Jot down a response to the prompt.

2. When you hear me say, "*Mingle, Mingle,*" move around the room with your response, a pencil or pen and notebook/ graphic organizer.

3. At the signal, pause and find a partner near you.

4. Share responses, listen actively and take notes.

SET UP THE ACTIVATOR

1. Explain the purpose of the Activator. You might say, *"The Activator we're going to do will offer you a chance to move around the room and share your ideas about _____ with different classmates. Talking with a variety of partners will sharpen your thinking, give you some new ideas and provide practice in being good listeners. And the movement will keep your brains alert so you can remember what you talked about."*

2. Review student directions.

3. Explain that students will receive prompts printed on different colored or numbered pieces of paper to help them see at-a-glance which prompt each classmate has. Tell students how many partners they will mingle with during the course of the Activator and how much time they will have with each one (one to two minutes).

4. Distribute a graphic organizer or tell students to use their notebooks to record their own responses and take notes on what classmates share.

MODEL AND TEACH

1. Model using different prompts than those in the Activator. Prior to modeling, jot down some notes in response to your prompt. Ask for a volunteer who is willing to help demonstrate this Activator, and give them time to prepare a response.

2. With the volunteer, model moving around the room with your notebook or graphic organizer, pen, and prompt, when you say *"Mingle, mingle, mingle."* Show students how to pause when the signal is given and find a partner with a different prompt.

3. Model sharing your response with the volunteer by referring to your notes and making eye contact rather than reading word for word. If students are showing each other an image or how they've worked out a problem, demonstrate how to hold the paper so that their partner can see it.

4. Ask the volunteer to share their thinking. Model responding by asking questions, paraphrasing or making connections.

5. If students are expected to take notes after talking with each partner, model doing this on the board by using symbols and abbreviations, and writing down key words or phrases.

6. Ask students what they noticed about moving around the room, sharing responses, and taking notes.

PRACTICE AND ASSESS

1. Distribute slips of paper with different prompts.

2. Give students one to two minutes of think time to jot down a response on their organizers or in their notebooks.

3. Ask students to stand up with a pen, their prompts, and graphic organizers or notebooks.

4. Say, "*Mingle, mingle, mingle*" and have students walk around the room. Encourage them to keep moving towards any empty space in the room. Provide the signal to stop and ask students to pair up with someone standing near them. Circulate to make sure that everyone has a partner.

5. Ask students to begin sharing their responses. Monitor and support students' active participation and learning.

6. Use a timer and indicate when time is halfway through, and encourage the other partner to begin responding if they haven't already done so.

7. Offer some feedback on ways students were interacting effectively with one another and remind them of any behaviors you would like them to practice in the next round. For example, "*I loved how you were asking questions of each other. In the next round I want to remind you to make eye contact when you're sharing your response, which will help you communicate effectively with your partner.*"

8. If you want students to take notes after each round, provide one to two minutes to do this now.

9. Ask students to thank their partners by name.

10. Say, "*Mingle, mingle, mingle*" to indicate that students should move around the room again.

11. Repeat the process two or three times with different partners.

12. Use a signal to get the group's attention and debrief by asking some of the following content and process questions:

Content questions
- What is something you heard about _____ that stood out to you?
- What is something about _____ that you realized or are wondering?
- In what ways did your understanding of _____ deepen or change from the beginning of the Activator to the end?

Process questions
- What was it like to do this Mix and Mingle Activator?
- If we were to do this Activator again, what suggestions might you make about what we could do the same or differently?

Thank students for their active participation, affirm understandings, and address any misconceptions that surfaced.

17

TROUBLESHOOTING TIPS

- If there is an uneven number of students, one pair can travel together.

- If students are reluctant to partner up on their own, suggest pairings as you circulate around the room.

VARIATIONS AND EXTENSIONS

- Display/project prompts on a slide, the board, or chart paper that **all** students respond to (see High-Performing Community of Learners examples below).

- Play music while students move around.

- Tell students to exchange slips after each round and explain their previous partner's slip and response to their new partner.

- Let students know ahead of time that you will do a cold call (select index cards or popsicle sticks with students' names) to hold students accountable for what they learned during the Activator.

- Prior to engaging in the Mix and Mingle Activator, create "expert groups" by having students with the same slip come to a shared understanding of what their text, quote, or image means.

- Ask students to find two to three others who have different slips. Have them sit down and share their thinking as a small group instead of walking around and changing partners.

- Differentiate the prompts, images or text, based upon readiness or interest.

Using Mix and Mingle to Create a High-Performing Community of Learners

Mix and Mingle Activators can build Trust and Belonging by forging connections between and among students and teachers. At the beginning of their language arts course, students can interview each other with self-created questions that they themselves might like to be asked, using the Mix and Mingle format. After several rounds of sharing and listening to responses, students discover commonalities and acknowledge differences that will ease them into working together more effectively throughout the year. Starting a course this way also sets a strong expectation that students will learn from each other as well as from the teacher, who is also a learner during this Activator. As the teacher circulates, they gather information about individual students that can be used to build and maintain relationships essential for learning.

Mix and Mingle is also a low-risk way of reflecting on Classroom Expectations in order to create a High-Performing Community of Learners. In a chemistry class, students might Mix and Mingle around the question: *"What is a Classroom Expectation that might be challenging for you to meet and what are some supports that might help you meet this challenge?"* In this way students unpack the chemistry teacher's Classroom Expectations by predicting roadblocks they might encounter and by problem solving around these. Engaging actively around Classroom Expectations encourages students to begin to internalize them, and as the teacher listens in, they learn what students need to meet them.

Mix and Mingle Examples for Creating a High-Performing Community of Learners

- If classmates were to ask you a question that would help them get to know you, what might they ask? Use this question to interview classmates.

- Select a Classroom Expectation that you know you will be successful with. What are some of the things you can do to meet this expectation? Select an expectation that might be challenging for you to meet. Explain the challenge and what supports might help you meet this expectation.

- What is something you learned from a peer this week? What is one way you helped out a peer this week?

Using Mix and Mingle to Support Learning in the Content Areas

Generate Connections to Prior Knowledge: Mix and Mingle offers an energizing way of helping students make connections to new content. Prior to launching into *Macbeth*, an English language arts teacher might make up slips with short character descriptions written in the first person along with key quotes for Macbeth, Lady Macbeth, Duncan, the Witches, Banquo and Macduff. After reading their slips and circling key phrases, students can Mix and Mingle, introduce themselves as their character, say and then "translate" their quote for their partners by making an inference about its meaning. For many students who are intimidated by Shakespeare, this is a fun and low-risk way to create prior knowledge about the play before they even crack open the text.

Provide Opportunities to Practice Skills and Deepen Understanding: As educators we know that the best way to learn something is by teaching it to somebody else. The Mix and Mingle Activator is a great vehicle for deepening students' understanding of content by having them teach it to a peer. The biology student who repeatedly explains the function of proteins strengthens their grasp of the concept with each new partner. And as they listen and take notes on what their classmates teach them about the function of nucleic acids, carbohydrates and lipids, their understanding of the other biological molecules grows.

17

Provide Opportunities for Formative Assessment: This Activator provides a critical opportunity for teachers to figure out what students know, understand and can do. A world language teacher can learn a lot by circulating and taking notes while her students carry cards with key vocabulary, show them to their partners, and ask in the target language, "*What is this?*" to which the classmate responds, "*That is a _____ .*" This enables a teacher to quickly pick up on patterns that will help her re-teach some vocabulary and determine which students might benefit from a more in-depth, small-group mini-lesson the next day.

Prepare Students for Assessments: Mix and Mingle prepares students for a final assessment by transforming them into tutors. When algebra students have to determine which solution is correct and explain this to a peer two or three times, they are storing this information in long-term memory before an end-of-unit exam. In order to ensure accuracy of student responses, the teacher might want to create "expert" groups where students collaboratively determine the correct answer prior to peer teaching during the Activator.

Inject Relevance Into the Curriculum: The highly interactive nature of this Activator makes it a natural bridge between the classroom and life outside. For example, geography students can participate in a Mix and Mingle Activator to share inferences about how a dramatic shift in population growth might impact everything from clean drinking water to housing in the future. Connecting geography to larger societal issues in this interactive way increases the likelihood of students reaching the learning outcome(s).

Math

Algebra

Examine the problem assigned to you and identify which is the correct solution and which is the error. Explain your response to your partners.

Problem #1: Convert $\sqrt{7x}$ to fractional components.

Solution A:
$$\sqrt{7x} = 7x\ 1/2$$

Solution B:
$$\sqrt{7x} = (7x)1/2$$

Problem #2: Solve for x: $x^2 - 7x + 3 = x^2 + 5x - 21$

Solution A:
$$x^2 - 7x + 3 = x^2 + 5x - 21$$
$$ - x^2 - x^2$$
$$-7x + 3 = 5x - 21$$
$$ -5x -5x$$
$$-12x + 3 = -21$$
$$ -3 -3$$
$$-12x = -24$$
$$-12 -12$$
$$x = -2$$

Solution B:
$$x^2 - 7x + 3 = x^2 + 5x - 21$$
$$ - x^2 - x^2$$
$$-7x + 3 = 5x - 21$$
$$ +7x +7x$$
$$3 = 12x - 21$$
$$ -3 -3$$
$$12x = -24$$
$$12 12$$
$$x = 2$$

Problem #3

Convert $(16x)^{3/2}$ to radical form.

Solution A
$$\sqrt{16^3}\ \sqrt{x^3} = \sqrt{4096}\ \sqrt{x^3} = 64\ \sqrt{x^3}$$

Solution **B**
$$((\sqrt{16})^3)^{1/2}\ \sqrt[3]{x^2} = (4096)^{1/2}\ \sqrt[3]{x^2} = 64\ \sqrt[3]{x^2}$$

17

Geometry

1.) Discuss and solve the problem with your partner (project problems on a screen if possible).

Write the expressions that would enable you to find the area of each circle.

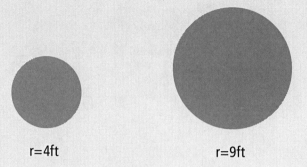

r=4ft   r=9ft

2.) Write the expressions that would enable you to find the circumference of each circle.

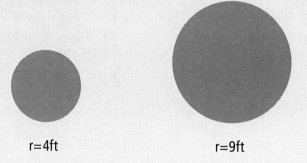

r=4ft   r=9ft

3.) Find the area of the entire shaded figure.

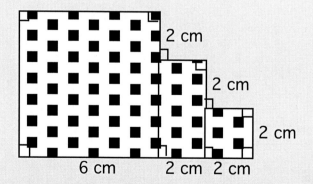

2 cm

2 cm

2 cm

6 cm   2 cm   2 cm

Science

Earth Science

In preparation for the end of unit assessment on Forces that Raise the Surface, quiz your classmates by asking the question assigned to you.

1.) How did the continents form?
2.) What causes earthquakes?
3.) What causes volcanoes to erupt?
4.) What's the difference between magma and lava?
5.) What caused mountains to form?

Biology

Explain the main function of your assigned biological molecules to each of your partners.

1.) Nucleic acids
2.) Proteins
3.) Carbohydrates
4.) Lipids

Chemistry

Explain the trend from the Periodic Table illustrated on your slip of paper and whether there is a decrease or increase down groups/columns and across rows and why.

1.) Atomic radius
2.) Electronegativity
3.) Ionization energy

Physics

With each of your partners, explain and discuss your response to the assigned question on the transmission of heat.

1.) When a hot object placed in contact with a cooler object warms the cooler object, can you say it loses as much temperature as the cooler one gains? Defend your answer.

2.) As more energy from fossil and other non-renewable fuels is consumed on earth, the overall temperature of the earth tends to rise. Regardless of the increase in energy, however, the temperature does not rise indefinitely. By what process is an indefinite rise prevented? Explain your answer.

3.) You can bring water in a paper cup to a boil by placing it over a hot flame. Why doesn't the paper cup burn?

4.) If you wish to save fuel on a cold day, and you're going to leave your warm house for a half hour or so, should you turn your thermostat down a few degrees, down all the way or leave it at room temperature?

17

Social Studies

Geography

The world's population is over seven billion and climbing. What are the ways this population shift will impact people and the earth? Hypothesize some of the short-term and long-term impacts of the category assigned to you and share your thinking with each of your partners

1.) Clean drinking water

2.) Gasoline/fuel/electricity

3.) Food waste/food availability

4.) Jobs

5.) Housing

6.) Pollution

7.) Human health (diseases and health care)

U.S. History

Share and analyze your political cartoon from 1875-1917 that illustrates America's rise as a world power. (Teacher identifies and prints copies of four to six political cartoons related to America's rise as a world power.)

World History

Explain the key event in the fight for Indian independence from Great Britain that is described on the card. (Teacher creates cards with information on six to eight key events from India's fight for independence.)

Government

Discuss with your partner some of the ways the case on your colored piece of paper impacted due process.

Pink Paper: *Gideon v. Wainwright*

Yellow Paper: *Escobedo v. Illinois*

Green Paper: *Miranda v. Arizona*

Round #1: Find someone with the same color paper as you/same court case.

Round #2: Find someone with a different color paper as you/different court case.

Round #3: Find someone with a color that you have not shared with yet/ different case.

English Language Arts

Writing

Explain your response to the following question to each of your partners:

Prior to writing a current events research paper:

If you were an investigative reporter, what is a hot topic in the news you might want to explore? What are some things you might want to find out?

Reading – Literature

Read the description of your assigned character from *Macbeth*. Then introduce yourselves as the character, and say and "translate" your quote for your partners.

1.) Macbeth
2.) Lady Macbeth
3.) Banquo
4.) Duncan
5.) Witches
6.) Macduff

Reading – Informational Texts

Discuss with your partner how your particular quote supports the author's claim that _____ .

Pink paper: Quote #1

Yellow paper: Quote #2

Blue paper: Quote #3

Green paper: Quote #4

(Teacher identifies informational text and creates four color-coded quote strips from text.)

Speaking and Listening

Identify and explain the use of ethos, logos or pathos in the excerpt from Dr. Martin Luther King, Jr.'s "I Have a Dream" speech on your slip of paper.

Pink slip: Logos

Blue paper: Pathos

Yellow paper: Ethos

Language

Share with your partners an inference about the meaning of the Greek root based upon the sample words on your slip of paper.

1.) bio (biology, biography)
2.) photo (photosynthesis, photograph)
3.) thermo (thermos, thermometer)
4.) scope (microscope, telescope)
5.) micro (microscope, microchip)

17

World Languages

Point to your picture that represents one key vocabulary word from our unit, and ask your partners in the target language, "*How do you say* _____ *?*" pointing to the picture. Each partner responds by saying "*That is a* _____ *.*"

Ask and tell each other about your families in (the target language).

Yellow slip: "*Who do you live with?*"

Blue slip: "*Do you have brothers or sisters? How old are they?*"

Pink slip: "*What is something your family likes to do together?*"

Ask and tell each other in (the target language) what you do on a typical Monday at the time of day that appears on your slip of paper.

Suggestions for Writing Your Own Rotation Stations Activators:

This is a great Activator to use if you teach a complex topic that requires students to build a lot of background knowledge. If you use a PowerPoint presentation with a lot of slides/visuals to teach background knowledge, consider turning part of it into a Rotation Stations Activator. If you teach a skill that you know students will need significant practice to master, create a Rotation Station Activator to support this practice and get ready to witness the benefits of injecting novelty, collaborative interaction, and physical movement into skills practice.

YOUR TURN

Design Your Own Rotation Stations Activators

A Checklist for Designing Effective Activators:

☐ *Does the prompt support a specific learning outcome?*

☐ *Is the prompt engaging?* Can students respond without feeling anxious or uncomfortable? Do students have enough prior knowledge to feel competent in their responses? Will the prompt ignite curiosity, make content relevant, and challenge students to think at a high level?

☐ *Is the prompt crafted with invitational language that promotes exploration and reduces the need for certainty?* Invitational prompts might begin with "What might…?" "What are some of the…?" or "What is your hunch for why…?"

17

CHAPTER

The new reality is that much of today's knowledge will be outdated soon; consequently, we need to teach not only facts and concepts but also the skills with which to learn; thinking critically and analytically, asking questions, formulating hypotheses, and collaboratively discussing options.

—Jackie A. Walsh and Beth D. Sattes

Developing a Plan

What might infusing Activators into your weekly instruction look like?

While we advocate using at least one Activator that includes movement in each lesson, we are all too familiar with the pressures on classroom teachers so we encourage you to consider your specific situation and determine how many and what types of Activators you can effectively and comfortably begin integrating into your teaching. An easy starting place might be to integrate at least one Turn and Talk into every lesson in places where you otherwise might have simply just called on someone who raised their hand. Another example would be to look at where you would review key concepts or vocabulary during a unit and integrate a Card Sort. Or you might kick off a unit by using Post It Up to solicit student background knowledge on the unit topic.

As we stressed earlier in the book, you want to make sure the Activators are meaningfully aligned with course and unit outcomes to ensure they add value to your lessons. So before deciding on which Activators to use, take a close look at your unit and see which ones might best align with the skills and content you are teaching. You might also consider starting with one or two of the foundational Activators and then, as you and your students feel more comfortable, integrate one or more complex Activators featured in later chapters.

Below are two examples for how a teacher might strategically plan to integrate at least three Activators into weekly lesson planning over the course of a six-week unit. These examples are designed to give teachers an idea of what it might look like to get started using Activators, whether they are planning for a new school year or looking to ramp up engagement in an existing class mid-year. Notice that in both cases there is an immediate injection of Activators to Create a High-Performing Community of Learners, followed by introducing four to five Activators over the first three weeks of the unit, and then repeating those same types of Activators two or more times throughout the unit. This is intentional—allowing both students and the teacher to become more efficient and skilled at each Activator in order to maximize its instructional impact.

EXAMPLE 1

Mr. Jackson's U.S. History class at the Beginning of the School Year

Week 1

To support a High-Performing Community of Learners:
- Name Tent Toss
- Common Ground
- Weather Report Wave (How was your first week of school?)

To support content instruction:
- Turn and Talk

Week 2

To support a High-Performing Community of Learners:
- Weather Report Wave (How is your day going?)

To support content instruction:
- Turn and Talk
- Four (or more) Corners

Week 3

To support content instruction:
- Turn and Talk
- Silent Conversation
- Four (or more) Corners

Week 4

To support content instruction:
- Toss One, Take One
- Turn and Talk
- Opinion Continuum

18

Week 5

To support content instruction:
- Silent Conversation
- Opinion Continuum
- Four (or more) Corners

Week 6

To support a High-Performing Community of Learners:
- Weather Report Wave (How are you feeling about the upcoming unit assessment?)

To support content instruction:
- Toss One, Take One
- Silent Conversation

EXAMPLE 2

Ms. Valentina's Geometry class, mid-year, hoping to ramp up student engagement

Week 1

To support a High-Performing Community of Learners:
- Moving Line-Up (What food item could you not live without? What is a hobby or a personal interest? Describe what it takes for you to be interested and engaged in a class/subject.)

To support content instruction:
- Turn and Talk

Week 2

To support a High-Performing Community of Learners:
- Turn and Talk (brainstorm Group Agreements)

To support content instruction:
- Mini Whiteboard
- Card Sorts

Week 3

To support content instruction:
- Turn and Talk
- Mini Whiteboard
- Post It Up

Week 4

To support a High-Performing Community of Learners:
- Post It Up (to review Group Agreements)

To support content instruction:
- Card Sort
- Mini Whiteboard

Week 5

To support content instruction:
- Turn and Talk
- Mini Whiteboard
- Post It Up

Week 6

To support content instruction:
- Post It Up
- Card Sort
- Mini Whiteboard

How might a teacher go about ritualizing the use of Activators in their weekly planning?

Another way to consider incorporating Activators in a systematic way is to ritualize an Activator to a specific day over the course of a four- to six-week unit. This rotating model provides both predictability and day-to-day novelty, supporting students to be in that optimal learning state of "relaxed alertness" (Caine et al., 2009). It also makes for streamlined planning on the part of teachers. When following this model it is important to select Activators that are highly flexible and easily matched to your unit content to ensure they are easily aligned to the daily lessons' outcomes.

Ritualized Use of Activators during a Four-Week English Unit on Point of View
- Monday: Popcorn
- Tuesday: Turn and Talk
- Wednesday: Silent Conversation
- Thursday: Post It Up
- Friday: Opinion Continuum

18

Collaborating Around Activators

For teachers who have collaboration time built into their schedules, we encourage you to bring Activators into your meetings and professional dialogues, talk about how you have or will implement various Activators, troubleshoot facilitation questions, and even invite each other into your classrooms to get feedback. You might consider reading and discussing the first three introductory chapters of the book and then each trying the same or a different Activator and reporting back to the group.

For teacher teams who teach the same cohort of students, consider identifying a consistent set of Activators to use across all of your subject areas. You might even strategically divide up those Activators so that each teacher is responsible for introducing one, giving them an opportunity to use one non-academic prompt that supports a High-Performing Community of Learners. This collaborative approach saves teachers time, establishes common expectations for participation, and maximizes learning as students have more opportunities to practice and become increasingly skilled and comfortable with each Activator in a variety of settings.

Where Will You Begin?

We champion Activators because we know the impact they can have on student learning and achievement. In our own classrooms, and in the classrooms we have visited around the country, we have witnessed the powerful effect Activators have on student engagement. So whether you start modestly by integrating an Activator once a week, or already use a variety of strategies and are looking for more to add to your toolbox, we hope this book serves to inspire you.

Glossary of Key Terms

Classroom Agreements: A negotiated set of behaviors and actions between the students and teacher about the ways in which the class will work and learn together. For example, students and the teacher might create Classroom Agreements that say, "*Let people finish what they have to say before someone else speaks. Share the talk space. Give everyone a chance to speak. Help each other out.*" For more information on creating Classroom Agreements please visit http://www.esrnational.org/activators.

Classroom Expectations: Beliefs that a teacher holds about what students are capable of doing and achieving. Examples include: "*I expect you to take responsibility for your learning. I expect you to challenge yourself. I expect you to make your best effort.*"

Cold Call: A questioning technique that makes engaged participation the expectation by calling on students by name regardless of whether they have raised their hands. When used regularly and with positivity, Cold Call increases attention and participation, provides formative assessment, strengthens individual accountability and supports effective pacing (Lemov, 2010).

Exit Ticket: A short, written response to a question or prompt at the end of class that students complete on a slip of paper and hand to the teacher before leaving. Exit Tickets allow students to reflect on what they have learned and serve as formative assessment that helps the teacher determine the extent to which students reached the intended learning outcome.

Essential Question: A question that students can examine continually in order to come to an understanding of key ideas and processes in a unit or course (McTighe & Wiggins, 2013). Examples include:

- Math—*When and why should I estimate?*
- Science—*How are structure and function related in living things?*
- Social Studies—*What is worth fighting for?*

- English Language Arts—*How do effective writers hook and hold their readers?*
- World Languages—*What should I do in my head when trying to learn a target language?*

Formative Assessment: Real-time reciprocal student-teacher feedback that enables teachers to assess students' skill acquisition and understanding, adjust and differentiate instruction according to learning needs, and provide corrective feedback so that students can close learning gaps and meet learning outcomes successfully.

Habits of Learning: A set of social and emotional competencies that support learning as well as personal, interpersonal, and group efficacy. These competencies become automatic through instruction, modeling, practice, and assessment and have a significant impact on students' achievement and their capacity to perform and function in the classroom community. Examples include: working cooperatively; sustaining focus; attention and effort; setting academic goals; and reflecting on and monitoring progress.

High-Performing Community of Learners; A group of students engaged in high-quality, challenging instruction and meaningful learning. In a High-Performing Community of Learners, students experience individual success, work effectively with peers and develop healthy relationships that result in a positive and personalized learning environment. Key to developing a High-Performing Community of Learners are: 1) building trust and belonging, 2) establishing and maintaining Classroom Expectations and Classroom Agreements, and 3) supporting Habits of Learning.

Instructional Supports: Specific prompts, cues, questions, coaching, and feedback that a teacher uses to elicit and sustain engagement in learning for all students. Examples include: use of a consistent signal to get attention for transitions, formative assessment, and clear instructions.

Learning Outcome: A statement that captures specifically what students should know and/or be able to do by the end of the lesson, series of lessons, unit, or course. We advocate for learning outcomes that are communicated clearly to students in student-friendly language. We also recognize that there are a variety of other terms such as learning objective, daily objective, target learning goal, or learning targets, all with varying definitions and criteria that are used by educators and schools around the country to specify the goals of student learning.

Learning Strategies: Students' specific actions that facilitate knowledge and skill acquisition to support effective, transferrable, and self-directed learning. Examples: Turn and Talk, Quick Jots, and Quick Draws.

Model, Teach, Practice, Assess: A generalized instructional approach for developing and using a skill competently. This approach emerges from the mastery learning movement and risk prevention research associated with social skill acquisition (Catalano, R.F. & Hawkins, J.D. 1996; Goldstein, A.P. 1981, 1988).

- **Model** is the "show me how" stage that demands attentive observation and listening.
- **Teach** includes introducing and defining the skill to be learned and outlining steps for doing the skill effectively.
- **Practice** involves performing the skill step by step, engaging in "out loud" rehearsal, and experiencing multiple opportunities to practice in multiple contexts.
- **Assess** incorporates self-reflection and peer and teacher feedback to monitor progress in demonstrating mastery of the skill.

Numbered Heads: A Kagan© learning strategy in which small group members count off so that each one has a number (1, 2, 3, or 4). The group works together to come to consensus on an answer to a question or solve a problem. Afterwards, the teacher randomly selects a number and calls on students with this number to explain their group's answer.

Quick Draw: Students demonstrate their understanding of an abstract term or concept by representing it in a drawing for one to three minutes (Himmele & Himmele 2009).

Quick Jot: Students reflect on what they're learning or thinking by writing down words, phrases, or sentences for one to three minutes.

Table Talk: An informal, small group conversation among three to five students sitting at a table.

Think Aloud: The teacher models a process for approaching a specific task by thinking out loud in front of the class and making their cognitive strategies evident. This instructional support helps students understand what strategies to employ when they approach the task on their own.

APPENDIX

Content Area Examples Common Core Alignment

The following two charts align the Activator content area examples presented in this book with the Common Core Standards for Mathematics and English Language Arts.

The Common Core State Standards Initiative's Standards for Mathematical Practice and Standards by Domain can be found at http://www.corestandards.org/Math.

The Common Core State Standards Initiative's English Language Arts College and Career Readiness Anchor Standards can be found at http://www.corestandards.org/ELA-Literacy.

We offer these charts as a planning tool for teachers who are in the process of designing or redesigning their courses and units to align with the Common Core State Standards and to illustrate how Activators can directly support various standards. Currently, common standards for science, social studies, and world languages have yet to be finalized or written. As such tools evolve, we will include them in future editions of *Activators*.

Activators Content Area Examples for Common Core State Standards for **Mathematics**

Grade Level Standards	Standards for Mathematical Practice	Prompt	Activator Format
CCSS.Math.Content.4.NF.C.5 Express a fraction with denominator 10 as an equivalent fraction with denominator 100, and use this technique to add two fractions with respective denominators 10 and 100.	None applicable	Match the equivalent percentage, fraction, and decimal.	Card Sorts

CCSS.Math.Content.4.NF.C.6 Use decimal notation for fractions with denominators 10 or 100.	None applicable	Match the equivalent percentage, fraction, and decimal.	Card Sorts
CCSS.Math.Content.7.G.B.4 Know the formulas for the area and circumference of a circle and use them to solve problems; give an informal derivation of the relationship between the circumference and area of a circle.	CCSS.Math.Practice.MP1 Make sense of problems and persevere in solving them. CCSS.Math.Practice.MP4 Model with mathematics. CCSS.Math.Practice.MP5 Use appropriate tools strategically.	Pairing #1: Write the expression that would enable you to find the area of the circle (see image on page 194). Pairing #2: Write the expression that would enable you to find the circumference of the circle (see image on page 194). Pairing #3: Find the area of the entire shaded figure (see image on page 194).	Mix and Mingle
CCSS.Math.Content.7.G.B.5 Use facts about supplementary, complementary, vertical, and adjacent angles in a multi-step problem to write and solve simple equations for an unknown angle in a figure.	CCSS.Math.Practice.MP1 Make sense of problems and persevere in solving them. CCSS.Math.Practice.MP4 Model with mathematics. CCSS.Math.Practice.MP5 Use appropriate tools strategically.	With your partner, determine which is the correct solution and which is the error. Explain your response to your partner. (See problems and possible solutions on page 161.)	Moving Line-Up
CCSS.Math.Content.7.G.B.6 Solve real-world and mathematical problems involving area, volume and surface area of two- and three-dimensional objects composed of triangles, quadrilaterals, polygons, cubes, and right prisms.	CCSS.Math.Practice.MP1 Make sense of problems and persevere in solving them. CCSS.Math.Practice.MP4 Model with mathematics. CCSS.Math.Practice.MP5 Use appropriate tools strategically.	Pairing #1: Write the expression that would enable you to find the area of the image (see circle on page 194). Pairing #2: Write the expression that would enable you to find the circumference of the circle (see image on page 194). Pairing #3: Find the area of the entire shaded figure (see image on page 194).	Mix and Mingle

CCSS.Math.Content.7.G.B.6	CCSS.Math.Practice.MP3	Agree or Disagree: Figure B holds more water than Figure A (see images of cylinders on page 128).	Opinion Continuum
Solve real-world and mathematical problems involving area, volume and surface area of two- and three-dimensional objects composed of triangles, quadrilaterals, polygons, cubes, and right prisms.	Construct viable arguments and critique the reasoning of others.		
CCSS.Math.Content.7.G.B.6	CCSS.Math.Practice.MP1	1. Solve each of the following equations for r.	Mini Whiteboard
Solve real-world and mathematical problems involving area, volume and surface area of two- and three-dimensional objects composed of triangles, quadrilaterals, polygons, cubes, and right prisms.	Make sense of problems and persevere in solving them.	$C = 2pr$ $A = pr2$	
	CCSS.Math.Practice.MP4	2. Jamie has a 2' x 4' pen for her guinea pigs but the mom is pregnant and she needs more space. She wants to make the pen six times as big as it is now.	
	Model with mathematics.	a) What should the dimensions of the new pen be?	
		b) Compare the perimeters of the two pens. How much more fencing will she need to buy?	
	CCSS.Math.Practice.MP5		
	Use appropriate tools strategically.	3. Find the area of the shaded region (see image on page 85).	
		4. Find the volume and surface area of the figures (see images on page 85).	
CCSS.Math.Content.8.EE.A.2	CCSS.Math.Practice.MP1	What is the length of the side of the triangle labeled m? Show all work (see image on page 73).	Silent Conversation
Use square root and cube root symbols to represent solutions to equations of the form $x2 = p$ and $x3 = p$, where p is a positive rational number. Evaluate square roots of small perfect squares and cube roots of small perfect cubes. Know that $\sqrt{2}$ is irrational.	Make sense of problems and persevere in solving them. CCSS.Math.Practice.MP3 Construct viable arguments and critique the reasoning of others.		

CCSS.Math.Content.8.EE.A.2	CCSS.Math.Practice.MP1	Both Jessie and Tammi are given the triangle shown at the right and are asked to find the length of c. Jessie says c = 31 while Tammi says c = 25 (see image on page 35). Who is correct? Explain completely and identify the error that led to the incorrect answer.	Turn and Talk/ Popcorn
Use square root and cube root symbols to represent solutions to equations of the form $x2 = p$ and $x3 = p$, where p is a positive rational number. Evaluate square roots of small perfect squares and cube roots of small perfect cubes. Know that $\sqrt{2}$ is irrational.	Make sense of problems and persevere in solving them. CCSS.Math.Practice.MP3 Construct viable arguments and critique the reasoning of others.		
CCSS.Math.Content.8.G.B.7 Apply the Pythagorean Theorem to determine unknown side lengths in right triangles in real-world and mathematical problems in two and three dimensions.	CCSS.Math.Practice.MP1 Make sense of problems and persevere in solving them. CCSS.Math.Practice.MP3 Construct viable arguments and critique the reasoning of others.	Both Jessie and Tammi are given the triangle shown at the right and are asked to find the length of c. Jessie says c = 31 while Tammi says c = 25 (see image on page 35). Who is correct? Explain completely and identify the error that led to the incorrect answer.	Turn and Talk/ Popcorn
CCSS.Math.Content.8.G.B.7 Apply the Pythagorean Theorem to determine unknown side lengths in right triangles in real-world and mathematical problems in two and three dimensions.	CCSS.Math.Practice.MP1 Make sense of problems and persevere in solving them. CCSS.Math.Practice.MP3 Construct viable arguments and critique the reasoning of others.	What is the length of the side of the triangle labeled m? Show all work. (See image on page 73.)	Silent Conversation
CCSS.Math.Content.8.G.C.9 Know the formulas for the volumes of cones, cylinders, and spheres and use them to solve real-world and mathematical problems.	CCSS.Math.Practice.MP5 Use appropriate tools strategically.	Move to a corner that represents one of the geometric solids, and work with a partner to find its volume (see images on page 138).	Four (or more) Corners
CCSS.Math.Content.8.G.C.9 Know the formulas for the volumes of cones, cylinders, and spheres and use them to solve real-world and mathematical problems.	None applicable	Match each picture of a geometric solid with its correct name, volume and surface area formulas (see images online at http://www. esrnational.org/activators).	Card Sorts

CCSS.Math.Content.HSN-RN.A.2 Rewrite expressions involving radicals and rational exponents using the properties of exponents.	CCSS.Math.Practice.MP1 Make sense of problems and persevere in solving them. CCSS.Math.Practice.MP4 Model with mathematics. CCSS.Math.Practice.MP5 Use appropriate tools strategically.	With your partner, determine which is the correct solution and which is the error. Explain your response to your partner (see problems and possible solutions on page 193).	Mix and Mingle
CCSS.Math.Content.HSA-APR.A.1 Understand that polynomials form a system analogous to the integers, namely, they are closed under the operations of addition, subtraction, and multiplication; add, subtract, and multiply polynomials.	CCSS.Math.Practice.MP1 Make sense of problems and persevere in solving them. CCSS.Math.Practice.MP4 Model with mathematics. CCSS.Math.Practice.MP5 Use appropriate tools strategically.	With your partner, determine which is the correct solution and which is the error. Explain your response to your partner (see problems and possible solutions on page 160).	Moving Line-Up
CCSS.Math.Content.HSA-APR.B.3 Identify zeros of polynomials when suitable factorizations are available, and use the zeros to construct a rough graph of the function defined by the polynomial.	CCSS.Math.Practice.MP1 Make sense of problems and persevere in solving them.	What is the degree of this polynomial function? What are some other possibilities?	Turn and Talk/ Popcorn

CCSS.Math.Content.HSA-CED.A.1	CCSS.Math.Practice.MP1	1. Write an equation for each of the lines (see images on page 84).	Mini Whiteboard
Create equations and inequalities in one variable and use them to solve problems. Include equations arising from linear and quadratic functions, and simple rational and exponential functions.	Make sense of problems and persevere in solving them.	2. Solve each of the following equations and show all work.	
	CCSS.Math.Practice.MP3		
	Construct viable arguments and critique the reasoning of others.	a) $x2 + x - 20 = 0$	
		b) $3x2 + 7x = -2$	
	CCSS.Math.Practice.MP4		
	Model with mathematics.	3. Solve each of the following equations.	
	CCSS.Math.Practice.MP5		
	Use appropriate tools strategically.	a) $\lvert 2x + 3 \rvert = 4$	
		b) $3(2x - 7) > 10x + 5$	
		c) $\lvert 2x - 3 \rvert = 13$	
CCSS.Math.Content.HSA-CED.A.1	CCSS.Math.Practice.MP1	1. The following word problems are all modeled by the equation $y = .5x+3$ if x represents the number of weeks, or $y=2x+3$ if x represents the number of months. Choose one, move to the designated "corner" and solve with a partner. (See page 138 for word problems.)	Four (or more) Corners
Create equations and inequalities in one variable and use them to solve problems. Include equations arising from linear and quadratic functions, and simple rational and exponential functions.	Make sense of problems and persevere in solving them.		
		2. Look at the functions around the room. Move to one and work with a partner to graph it without a graphing calculator and identify the type of function it is.	
		a) $y = \frac{1}{2} x + 4$	
		b) $y = -x$	
		c) $y = x + 4$	
		d) $y = x+3$	
		e) $y = 2x - 5$	
		f) $y = 7$	
		g) $x = -2$	

CCSS.Math.Content.HSA-REI.A.1	CCSS.Math.Practice.MP1	Solve for x with your partner.	Silent Conversation
Explain each step in solving a simple equation as following from the equality of numbers asserted at the previous step, starting from the assumption that the original equation has a solution. Construct a viable argument to justify a solution method.	Make sense of problems and persevere in solving them. CCSS.Math.Practice.MP3 Construct viable arguments and critique the reasoning of others.	$4x + 7 = 10 + x$ $x2 + 7x + 12 = 0$ $x2 - x - 20 = 0$ $x2 - 7x = -10$	
CCSS.Math.Content.HSA-REI.A.1 Explain each step in solving a simple equation as following from the equality of numbers asserted at the previous step, starting from the assumption that the original equation has a solution. Construct a viable argument to justify a solution method.	CCSS.Math.Practice.MP1 Make sense of problems and persevere in solving them. CCSS.Math.Practice.MP3 Construct viable arguments and critique the reasoning of others. CCSS.Math.Practice.MP4 Model with mathematics. CCSS.Math.Practice.MP5 Use appropriate tools strategically.	1. Write an equation for each of the lines (see images on page 84). 2. Solve each of the following equations and show all work. a) $x2 + x - 20 = 0$ b) $3x2 + 7x = -2$ 3. Solve each of the following equations. a) $|2x + 3| = 4$ b) $3(2x - 7) > 10x + 5$ c) $|2x - 3| = 13$	Mini Whiteboard
CCSS.Math.Content.HSA-REI.B.3 Solve linear equations and inequalities in one variable, including equations with coefficients represented by letters.	CCSS.Math.Practice.MP1 Make sense of problems and persevere in solving them. CCSS.Math.Practice.MP3 Construct viable arguments and critique the reasoning of others.	Solve for x with your partner. $4x + 7 = 10 + x$ $x2 + 7x + 12 = 0$ $x2 - x - 20 = 0$ $x2 - 7x = -10$	Silent Conversation

CCSS.Math.Content.HSA-REI.B.3	CCSS.Math.Practice.MP1	1. Write an equation for each of the lines (see images on page 84).	Mini Whiteboard
Solve linear equations and inequalities in one variable, including equations with coefficients represented by letters.	Make sense of problems and persevere in solving them. CCSS.Math.Practice.MP3 Construct viable arguments and critique the reasoning of others.	2. Solve each of the following equations and show all work. a) $x2 + x - 20 = 0$ b) $3x2 + 7x = -2$	
	CCSS.Math.Practice.MP4 Model with mathematics. CCSS.Math.Practice.MP5 Use appropriate tools strategically.	3. Solve each of the following equations. a) $\mid 2x + 3 \mid = 4$ b) $3(2x - 7) > 10x + 5$ c) $\mid 2x - 3 \mid = 13$	
CCSS.Math.Content.HSA-REI.B.3	CCSS.Math.Practice.MP1	1. Solve each of the following equations for r.	Mini Whiteboard
Solve linear equations and inequalities in one variable, including equations with coefficients represented by letters.	Make sense of problems and persevere in solving them. CCSS.Math.Practice.MP4 Model with mathematics. CCSS.Math.Practice.MP5 Use appropriate tools strategically.	a) $C = 2pr$ b) $A = pr2$ 2. Jamie has a 2' x 4' pen for her guinea pigs but the mom is pregnant and she needs more space. She wants to make the pen six times as big as it is now. a) What should the dimensions of the new pen be? b) Compare the perimeters of the two pens. How much more fencing will she need to buy? 3. Find the area of the shaded region (see image on page 85). 4. Find the volume and surface area of the figures (see figures on page 85).	

CCSS.Math.Content.HSA-REI.B.3 Solve linear equations and inequalities in one variable, including equations with coefficients represented by letters.	CCSS.Math.Practice.MP1 Make sense of problems and persevere in solving them. CCSS.Math.Practice.MP4 Model with mathematics. CCSS.Math.Practice.MP5 Use appropriate tools strategically.	With your partner, determine which is the correct solution and which is the error. Explain your response to your partner (see problems and possible solutions on page 193).	Mix and Mingle
CCSS.Math.Content.HSA-REI.B.4b Solve quadratic equations by inspection (e.g., for $x2 = 49$), taking square roots, completing the square, the quadratic formula and factoring, as appropriate to the initial form of the equation. Recognize when the quadratic formula gives complex solutions and write them as $a \pm bi$ for real numbers a and b.	CCSS.Math.Practice.MP1 Make sense of problems and persevere in solving them. CCSS.Math.Practice.MP3 Construct viable arguments and critique the reasoning of others. CCSS.Math.Practice.MP4 Model with mathematics. CCSS.Math.Practice.MP5 Use appropriate tools strategically.	1. Write an equation for each of the lines (see images on page 84). 2. Solve each of the following equations and show all work. a) $x2 + x - 20 = 0$ b) $3x2 + 7x = -2$ 3. Solve each of the following equations. a) $\lvert 2x + 3 \rvert = 4$ b) $3(2x - 7) > 10x + 5$ c) $\lvert 2x - 3 \rvert = 13$	Mini Whiteboard
CCSS.Math.Content.HSA-REI.B.4b Solve quadratic equations by inspection (e.g., for $x2 = 49$), taking square roots, completing the square, the quadratic formula and factoring, as appropriate to the initial form of the equation. Recognize when the quadratic formula gives complex solutions and write them as $a \pm bi$ for real numbers a and b.	CCSS.Math.Practice.MP1 Make sense of problems and persevere in solving them. CCSS.Math.Practice.MP3 Construct viable arguments and critique the reasoning of others.	Solve for x with your partner. $4x + 7 = 10 + x$ $x2 + 7x + 12 = 0$ $x2 - x - 20 = 0$ $x2 - 7x = -10$	Silent Conversation

CCSS.Math.Content.HSA-REI.C.5 Prove that, given a system of two equations in two variables, replacing one equation by the sum of that equation and a multiple of the other produces a system with the same solutions.	CCSS.Math.Practice.MP1 Make sense of problems and persevere in solving them. CCSS.Math.Practice.MP3 Construct viable arguments and critique the reasoning of others.	Place a dot on the method you would use to solve for this system of equations (see methods on page 60). $y = -3x - 7$ $-5x + y = 1$	Post It Up
CCSS.Math.Content.HSA-REI.C.5 Prove that, given a system of two equations in two variables, replacing one equation by the sum of that equation and a multiple of the other produces a system with the same solutions.	CCSS.Math.Practice.MP1 Make sense of problems and persevere in solving them. CCSS.Math.Practice.MP3 Construct viable arguments and critique the reasoning of others.	Which method do you prefer for solving this system of linear equations algebraically? Show your work and explain your reasons for preferring this method. $\begin{cases} y = 2x + 4 \\ 3x + y = 9 \end{cases}$	Toss One, Take One
CCSS.Math.Content.HSA-REI.C.6 Solve systems of linear equations exactly and approximately (e.g., with graphs), focusing on pairs of linear equations in two variables.	CCSS.Math.Practice.MP1 Make sense of problems and persevere in solving them. CCSS.Math.Practice.MP3 Construct viable arguments and critique the reasoning of others.	Place a dot on the method you would use to solve for this system of equations (see methods on page 60). $y = -3x - 7$ $-5x + y = 1$	Post It Up
CCSS.Math.Content.HSA-REI.C.6 Solve systems of linear equations exactly and approximately (e.g., with graphs), focusing on pairs of linear equations in two variables.	CCSS.Math.Practice.MP3 Construct viable arguments and critique the reasoning of others.	Agree or Disagree: The substitution method is more efficient than the elimination method to solve this system of equations: $y = 2x + 4$ $3x + y = 9$	Opinion Continuum
CCSS.Math.Content.HSF-IF.A.1 Understand that a function from one set (called the domain) to another set (called the range) assigns to each element of the domain exactly one element of the range. If f is a function and x is an element of its domain, then $f(x)$ denotes the output of f corresponding to the input x. The graph of f is the graph of the equation $y = f(x)$.	CCSS.Math.Practice.MP4 Model with mathematics.	x-y table or x-y axes? Undefined slope or no slope? 3rd degree or 4th degree function? Function or relation?	Are You More Like

CCSS.Math.Content.HSF-IF.C.8b Use the properties of exponents to interpret expressions for exponential functions. For example, identify percent rate of change in functions such as y = (1.02)t, y = (0.97)t, y = (1.01)12t, y = (1.2)t/10, and classify them as representing exponential growth or decay.	None applicable	Logarithms Review (see station problems on page 176).	Rotation Stations
CCSS.Math.Content.HSG-MG.A.1 Use geometric shapes, their measures, and their properties to describe objects (e.g., modeling a tree trunk or a human torso as a cylinder).	CCSS.Math.Practice.MP4 Model with mathematics.	Sphere or pyramid? 2-D or 3-D figure? Regular or irregular polygon? Concave or convex polygon?	Are You More Like
CCSS.Math.Content.HSG-MG.A.2 Apply concepts of density based on area and volume in modeling situations (e.g., persons per square mile, BTUs per cubic foot).	CCSS.Math.Practice.MP3 Construct viable arguments and critique the reasoning of others.	Agree or Disagree: Figure B holds more water than Figure A (see images on page 128).	Opinion Continuum
CCSS.Math.Content.HSG-CO.A.5 Given a geometric figure and a rotation, reflection, or translation, draw the transformed figure using, e.g., graph paper, tracing paper, or geometry software. Specify a sequence of transformations that will carry a given figure onto another.		Compositions of Transformations (see problems on page 177).	Rotation Stations

Activators Content Area Examples for Common Core State Standards for **English Language Arts**

ELA Anchor Standard	Prompt	Activator Format
CCSS.ELA.Literacy.CCRA.R.1 Read closely to determine what the text says explicitly and to make logical inferences from it; cite specific textual evidence when writing or speaking to support conclusions drawn from the text.	What are some ways the text answers the essential question, _____ ?	Turn and Talk
CCSS.ELA.Literacy.CCRA.R.1 Read closely to determine what the text says explicitly and to make logical inferences from it; cite specific textual evidence when writing or speaking to support conclusions drawn from the text.	Respond to text-based questions about the *New York Times article*, "On Road to Recovery, Past Adversity Provides a Map" (see questions on page 164).	Moving Line-Up
CCSS.ELA.Literacy.CCRA.R.1 Read closely to determine what the text says explicitly and to make logical inferences from it; cite specific textual evidence when writing or speaking to support conclusions drawn from the text.	Discuss and respond to the artifacts at each station connected to *Grapes of Wrath* that will help you generate prior knowledge about the novel's setting and theme (see station artifacts on page 181).	Rotation Stations
CCSS.ELA.Literacy.CCRA.R.1 Read closely to determine what the text says explicitly and to make logical inferences from it; cite specific textual evidence when writing or speaking to support conclusions drawn from the text.	Read the description of your assigned character from *Macbeth.* Then introduce yourself as the character, and say and "translate" your quote for your partners.	Mix and Mingle
CCSS.ELA.Literacy.CCRA.R2 Determine central ideas or themes of a text and analyze their development; summarize the key supporting details and ideas.	Share your sentence summary of Chapter 4 of *Roll of Thunder, Hear My Cry* using the Somebody/Wanted/But/So framework.	Popcorn/Wave
CCSS.ELA.Literacy.CCRA.R2 Determine central ideas or themes of a text and analyze their development; summarize the key supporting details and ideas.	A headline of five words or less that captures a key idea in _____ .	Popcorn/Wave
CCSS.ELA.Literacy.CCRA.R.2 Determine central ideas or themes of a text and analyze their development; summarize the key supporting details and ideas.	What does it mean to be American?	Silent Conversation
CCSS.ELA.Literacy.CCRA.R.2 Determine central ideas or themes of a text and analyze their development; summarize the key supporting details and ideas.	Create an alternate title for Chapter _____ in _____ .	Mini Whiteboard
CCSS.ELA.Literacy.CCRA.R.2 Determine central ideas or themes of a text and analyze their development; summarize the key supporting details and ideas.	Pick a card that represents a central idea in The Gettysburg Address.	Image Cards

CCSS.ELA.Literacy.CCRA.R.2 Determine central ideas or themes of a text and analyze their development; summarize the key supporting details and ideas.	Process the feature article you read about _____ by completing a task at each station as a group (see station tasks on page 182).	Rotation Stations
CCSS.ELA.Literacy.CCRA.R.2 Determine central ideas or themes of a text and analyze their development; summarize the key supporting details and ideas.	Select a theme from *In the Time of the Butterflies* and talk with a partner about how this theme is developed in the novel (see themes on page 140).	Four (or more) Corners
CCSS.ELA.Literacy.CCRA.R.3 Analyze how and why individuals, events, or ideas develop and interact over the course of a text.	What are some ways that Gogol tries to remake his identity in the novel *The Namesake*?	Turn and Talk
CCSS.ELA.Literacy.CCRA.R3 Analyze how and why individuals, events, or ideas develop and interact over the course of a text.	What might be "wrong" with Holden? What are some pieces of evidence you might use to support your claim? (during a unit on *Catcher in the Rye*)	Silent Conversation
CCSS.ELA.Literacy.CCRA.R.3 Analyze how and why individuals, events, or ideas develop and interact over the course of a text.	Sequence 5-7 key events in _____.	Card Sorts
CCSS.ELA.Literacy.CCRA.R.3 Analyze how and why individuals, events, or ideas develop and interact over the course of a text.	What's a headline of seven words or less or a tweet that captures the essence of the conflict between Troy and Cory in Act 1, Scene 3 of *Fences*?	Toss One, Take One
CCSS.ELA.Literacy.CCRA.R.3 Analyze how and why individuals, events, or ideas develop and interact over the course of a text.	Was learning how to read a blessing or a curse for Frederick Douglass? Why?	Toss One, Take One
CCSS.ELA.Literacy.CCRA.R.3 Analyze how and why individuals, events, or ideas develop and interact over the course of a text.	Pick a card that represents one of Walter's character traits in *A Raisin in the Sun*.	Image Cards
CCSS.ELA.Literacy.CCRA.R.3 Analyze how and why individuals, events, or ideas develop and interact over the course of a text.	Hamlet or Laertes?	Are You More Like
CCSS.ELA.Literacy.CCRA.R.4 Interpret words and phrases as they are used in a text, including determining technical, connotative, and figurative meanings, and analyze how specific word choices shape meaning or tone.	What are three or four words from Lincoln's Second Inaugural Address that seem important, surprising, or symbolic to you?	Mini Whiteboard
CCSS.ELA.Literacy.CCRA.R5 Analyze the structure of texts, including how specific sentences, paragraphs, and larger portions of the text (e.g., a section, chapter, scene, or stanza) relate to each other and the whole.	Put a Post-it next to the sign that represents your response to the following statement: "The conflict in the novel *47* is unresolved at the end" (see options on page 62).	Post It Up

CCSS.ELA.Literacy.CCRA.R5 Analyze the structure of texts, including how specific sentences, paragraphs, and larger portions of the text (e.g., a section, chapter, scene, or stanza) relate to each other and the whole.	Put a Post-it next to the component that would be most helpful to you in reading a chapter in your science or social studies textbook (see options on page 63).	Post It Up
CCSS.ELA.Literacy.CCRA.R.5 Analyze the structure of texts, including how specific sentences, paragraphs, and larger portions of the text (e.g., a section, chapter, scene, or stanza) relate to each other and the whole.	Discuss with your partner how the quote supports the author's claim that _____ .	Mix and Mingle
CCSS.ELA.Literacy.CCRA.R.6 Assess how point of view or purpose shapes the content and style of a text.	Stand next to a sign representing one of the four freedoms included in Roosevelt's 1941 State of the Union address. Talk to a partner about Roosevelt's reasons for including this freedom in his speech.	Four (or more) Corners
CCSS.ELA.Literacy.CCRA.R.7 Integrate and evaluate content presented in diverse media and formats, including visually and quantitatively, as well as in words.	The novel *The Hunger Games* is better than the film.	Opinion Continuum
CCSS.ELA.Literacy.CCRA.R.8 Delineate and evaluate the argument and specific claims in a text, including the validity of the reasoning as well as the relevance and sufficiency of the evidence.	Sort claims that are supported by facts, reasons, and evidence, and those that are not in Winston Churchill's "Blood, Sweat and Tears" speech.	Card Sorts
CCSS.ELA.Literacy.CCRA.R.9 Analyze how two or more texts address similar themes or topics in order to build knowledge or to compare the approaches the authors take.	Olive Branch Petition or Declaration of Independence?	Are You More Like
CCSS.ELA.Literacy.CCRA.W.1 Write arguments to support claims in an analysis of substantive topics or texts using valid reasoning and relevant and sufficient evidence.	Put a star next to an aspect of your persuasive speech that you are feeling good about, and an exclamation point next to an aspect of your persuasive speech that you are feeling challenged by.	Post It Up
CCSS.ELA.Literacy.CCRA.W.1 Write arguments to support claims in an analysis of substantive topics or texts using valid reasoning and relevant and sufficient evidence.	Teenagers should be allowed to vote.	Opinion Continuum
CCSS.ELA.Literacy.CCRA.W.1 Write arguments to support claims in an analysis of substantive topics or texts using valid reasoning and relevant and sufficient evidence.	What is your editorial's claim and what are two pieces of supporting evidence? What is your editorial's claim and what are two counterclaims to yours? What is your editorial's claim? What is one counterclaim? Name a strength and a limit to this counterclaim.	Moving Line-Up

CCSS.ELA.Literacy.CCRA.W.1 Write arguments to support claims in an analysis of substantive topics or texts using valid reasoning and relevant and sufficient evidence.	Brainstorm relevant evidence to develop the claim as well as counterclaims at each station.	Rotation Stations
CCSS.ELA.Literacy.CCRA.W3 Write narratives to develop real or imagined experiences or events using effective technique, well-chosen details and well-structured event sequences.	What is a sensory detail you used in order to create an image for your readers?	Popcorn/Wave
CCSS.ELA.Literacy.CCRA.W.3 Write narratives to develop real or imagined experiences or events using effective technique, well-chosen details and well-structured event sequences.	Stand next to a sign that represents something you accomplished in your second draft of your narrative. Bring your draft and share with your partner what you accomplished.	Four (or more) Corners
CCSS.ELA.Literacy.CCRA.W.4 Produce clear and coherent writing in which the development, organization, and style are appropriate to task, purpose, and audience.	Sort the transition words into categories: similarity, contrast, sequence, examples, effect, conclusion.	Card Sorts
CCSS.ELA.Literacy.CCRA.W.4 Produce clear and coherent writing in which the development, organization, and style are appropriate to task, purpose, and audience.	Feature article or editorial?	Are You More Like
CCSS.ELA-Literacy.CCRA.W.5 Develop and strengthen writing as needed by planning, revising, editing, rewriting, or trying a new approach.	What are some strengths of the sample essay? What are some things you might suggest the writer focus on in the next draft?	Turn and Talk
CCSS.ELA.Literacy.CCRA.W.5 Develop and strengthen writing as needed by planning, revising, editing, rewriting, or trying a new approach.	Pick a card that represents one way you plan to revise the first draft of your memoir.	Image Cards
CCSS.ELA.Literacy.CCRA.W.7 Conduct short as well as more sustained research projects based on focused questions, demonstrating understanding of the subject under investigation.	Explain your response to the following question to each of your partners: If you were an investigative reporter, what is a hot topic in the news you might want to explore? What are some things you might want to find out?	Mix and Mingle
CCSS.ELA.Literacy.CCRA.W.8 Gather relevant information from multiple print and digital sources, assess the credibility and accuracy of each source, and integrate the information while avoiding plagiarism.	What are some search term words you might use to identify the book requested in the posting from a social network site (see posting on page 87)?	Mini Whiteboard

CCSS.ELA.Literacy.CCRA.W.8 Gather relevant information from multiple print and digital sources, assess the credibility and accuracy of each source, and integrate the information while avoiding plagiarism.	What are some ways you can determine the credibility of a website?	Toss One, Take One
CCSS.ELA.Literacy.CCRA.W.9 Draw evidence from literary or informational texts to support analysis, reflection, and research.	Prior to writing a literary essay, create a dialogue of authors: George Orwell and William Golding discussing what *Lord of The Flies* and *Shooting an Elephant* reveal about human nature (each student writes from the point-of-view of one of the authors).	Silent Conversation
CCSS.ELA.Literacy.CCRA.SL.1 Prepare for and participate effectively in a range of conversations and collaborations with diverse partners, building on others' ideas and expressing their own clearly and persuasively.	What is a question you might offer to jumpstart our conversation about _____ ?	Popcorn/Wave
CCSS.ELA.Literacy.CCCRA.SL.1 Prepare for and participate effectively in a range of conversations and collaborations with diverse partners, building on others' ideas and expressing their own clearly and persuasively.	Put a green dot by one thing you did really well during today's discussion and put a blue dot by one thing you want to be more intentional in practicing next time (see options on page 63).	Post It Up
CCSS.ELA.Literacy.CCRA.SL.1 Prepare for and participate effectively in a range of conversations and collaborations with diverse partners, building on others' ideas and expressing their own clearly and persuasively.	What is one point of agreement you heard in our discussion of the Internet's impact on gender stereotypes? What is one point of disagreement you heard in our discussion of the Internet's impact on gender stereotypes?	Mini Whiteboard
CCSS.ELA.Literacy.CCRA.SL.1 Prepare for and participate effectively in a range of conversations and collaborations with diverse partners, building on others' ideas and expressing their own clearly and persuasively.	Sort qualities of debate vs. dialogue.	Card Sorts
CCSS.ELA.Literacy.CCRA.SL.1 Prepare for and participate effectively in a range of conversations and collaborations with diverse partners, building on others' ideas and expressing their own clearly and persuasively.	What was one thing people agreed on during the discussion? What was one thing people disagreed about?	Toss One, Take One
CCSS.ELA.Literacy.CCRA.SL.1 Prepare for and participate effectively in a range of conversations and collaborations with diverse partners, building on others' ideas and expressing their own clearly and persuasively.	Pick a card that represents a key idea from your literature circle's discussion of _____ .	Image Cards

CCSS.ELA.Literacy.CCRA.SL.1	Dialogue or debate?	Are You More Like
Prepare for and participate effectively in a range of conversations and collaborations with diverse partners, building on others' ideas and expressing their own clearly and persuasively.		
CCSS.ELA.Literacy.CCRA.SL.3	Identify a type of rhetoric the speaker used and the impact it had on you as a listener.	Turn and Talk
Evaluate a speaker's point of view, reasoning, and use of evidence and rhetoric.		
CCSS.ELA.Literacy.CCRA.SL.3	The president offered sound arguments in his demand for a vote on gun control in his State of the Union address.	Opinion Continuum
Evaluate a speaker's point of view, reasoning, and use of evidence and rhetoric.		
CCSS.ELA.Literacy.CCRA.SL.3	What are some ways you would describe the speaker's point of view? What supporting evidence did the speaker offer to support her point of view? What might be examples of distorted or exaggerated evidence that the speaker used?	Moving Line-Up
Evaluate a speaker's point of view, reasoning, and use of evidence and rhetoric.		
CCSS.ELA.Literacy.CCRA.SL.3	Logical Fallacy Stations: Review definitions and examples of logical fallacies and post your own examples on chart paper (see examples on page 182).	Rotation Stations
Evaluate a speaker's point of view, reasoning, and use of evidence and rhetoric.		
CCSS.ELA.Literacy.CCRA.SL.3	Identify and explain the use of ethos, logos or pathos in the excerpt from Dr. Martin Luther King Jr.'s "I Have a Dream" speech on your slip of paper.	Mix and Mingle
Evaluate a speaker's point of view, reasoning, and use of evidence and rhetoric.		
CCSS.ELA.Literacy.CCRA.SL.6	Think of a time when you changed the way you normally speak. Stand next to the sign that represents a reason why you might have adapted your speech in this situation (see options on page 141).	Four (or more) Corners
Adapt speech to a variety of contexts and communicative tasks, demonstrating command of formal English when indicated or appropriate.		
CCSS.ELA.Literacy.CCRA.L.1	What are some ways of changing the following sentence to make it gender-neutral? "If a student studies hard, he will succeed."	Turn and Talk
Demonstrate command of the conventions of standard English grammar and usage when writing and speaking.		
CCSS.ELA.Literacy.CCRA.L.2	Place your Post-it along the continuum (strongly agree/strongly disagree) in a position that represents your response to the following statement: "I can distinguish between when I need to use a semicolon (;) and when I need to use a colon (:) in a sentence."	Post It Up
Demonstrate command of the conventions of standard English capitalization, punctuation, and spelling when writing.		
CCSS.ELA.Literacy.CCRA.L.2	Conventions Editing Stations: edit the anonymous student examples of convention errors found at each station.	Rotation Stations
Demonstrate command of the conventions of standard English capitalization, punctuation, and spelling when writing.		

CCSS.ELA.Literacy.CCRA.L.4 Determine or clarify the meaning of unknown and multiple-meaning words and phrases by using context clues, analyzing meaningful word parts, and consulting general and specialized reference materials, as appropriate.	Using context clues, draw a sketch that represents the meaning of the word _____ .	Mini Whiteboard
CCSS.ELA.Literacy.CCRA.L.4 Determine or clarify the meaning of unknown and multiple-meaning words and phrases by using context clues, analyzing meaningful word parts, and consulting general and specialized reference materials, as appropriate.	Match Latin roots with meaning.	Card Sorts
CCSS.ELA.Literacy.CCRA.L.4 Determine or clarify the meaning of unknown and multiple-meaning words and phrases by using context clues, analyzing meaningful word parts, and consulting general and specialized reference materials, as appropriate.	Use the context of the sentence to determine the meaning of the italicized word. Explain your thinking.	Toss One, Take One
CCSS.ELA.Literacy.CCRA.L.4 Determine or clarify the meaning of unknown and multiple-meaning words and phrases by using context clues, analyzing meaningful word parts, and consulting general and specialized reference materials, as appropriate.	The best way to figure out the meaning of a word is to look it up.	Opinion Continuum
CCSS.ELA.Literacy.CCRA.L.4 Determine or clarify the meaning of unknown and multiple-meaning words and phrases by using context clues, analyzing meaningful word parts, and consulting general and specialized reference materials, as appropriate.	Share with your partners an inference about the meaning of the Greek root based upon the sample words on your slip of paper.	Mix and Mingle
CCSS.ELA.Literacy.CCRA.L.4 Determine or clarify the meaning of unknown and multiple-meaning words and phrases by using context clues, analyzing meaningful word parts, and consulting general and specialized reference materials, as appropriate.	Stand next to the number that you consider to be the best meaning of the word _____ based upon sentence context.	Four (or more) Corners
CCSS.ELA.Literacy.CCRA.L.5 Demonstrate understanding of figurative language, word relationships, and nuances in word meanings.	Pick a card that represents a connotation of the word _____ .	Image Cards

CCSS.ELA.Literacy.CCRA.L.5 Demonstrate understanding of figurative language, word relationships, and nuances in word meanings.	Denotation or connotation?	Are You More Like
CCSS.ELA.Literacy.CCRA.L.5 Demonstrate understanding of figurative language, word relationships, and nuances in word meanings.	After reading Judith Ortiz Cofer's poem "The Latin Deli: An Ars Poetica," make inferences about what the speaker is trying to convey and figures of speech used (see questions on page 165).	Moving Line-Up
CCSS.ELA-Literacy.CCRA.L.6 Acquire and use accurately a range of general academic and domain-specific words and phrases sufficient for reading, writing, speaking, and listening at the college and career readiness level; demonstrate independence in gathering vocabulary knowledge when encountering an unknown term important to comprehension or expression.	What are some examples of subjective writing?	Popcorn/Wave
CCSS.ELA.Literacy.CCRA.L.6 Acquire and use accurately a range of general academic and domain-specific words and phrases sufficient for reading, writing, speaking, and listening at the college and career readiness level; demonstrate independence in gathering vocabulary knowledge when encountering an unknown term important to comprehension or expression.	Use seven of our unit's vocabulary words accurately in a silent dialogue using one of the scenarios (see scenarios on page 75).	Silent Conversation

Sample Habits of Learning

Habits of Participation

- I work cooperatively with others and do my fair share of work.
- I'm friendly, helpful, courteous and good-humored with others.

Habits of Work

- I follow directions and ask questions when I don't understand.
- I attempt each part of the task, assignment or test.

Habits of Discipline

- I sustain my focus, pay attention and persist in my effort until I "get it."
- I handle mistakes, setbacks, anger and frustration constructively.

Habits of Communication

- I share my thoughts and ideas in small and large groups.
- I use positive, non-aggressive language to express myself, ask for help and get what I need.

Habits of Mind

- I set academic goals and reflect on and monitor my progress.
- I'm curious and ask questions to probe for deeper understanding.

For more extensive information on supporting Habits of Learning, refer to Carol Miller Lieber's *Getting Classroom Management Right: Guided Discipline and Personalized Support in Secondary Schools,* page 130 (Educators for Social Responsibility, 2009).

Grouping Strategies

Teachers often group students in various ways depending on the structure of a particular Activator. Here are strategies for grouping students randomly, providing parameters for students to form their own groups, and grouping students using academic content.

Random Grouping Strategies

Counting Off

For example, to make nine groups of three in a class of twenty-seven, have students count off from one to nine three times. Then have all the ones, twos, threes (and so on) come together as groups.

Playing Cards

Give each student a card and ask them to find two or three other students that have the same number.

Puzzle Pieces or Pictures

Cut postcards or pictures into pieces, or create puzzle pieces using index cards. Distribute the pieces, and ask students to move around the room looking for others whose pieces complete the picture or puzzle.

Luck of the Draw

Have index cards with a different student's name on each one. Shuffle and pull cards randomly to form pairs, trios, or groups of four.

Providing Parameters for Students to Form their Own Groups

Ask students to form groups of three or four that include at least (choose two or three of the following categories):

- one person who is male
- one person who is female
- one person who is an oldest sibling
- one person who is a youngest sibling
- one person who was born between January and June
- one person who was born between July and December
- two people who are of different racial or ethnic origins
- one person who owns a pet and one who doesn't
- one person who _____ (make up your own)

Grouping Students Based on Academic Content

Create groups of cards based on your content area. Students can match the cards to form groups.

Some examples include:

Math:
- Pairs: two equations that share the same answer
- Trios: three equations that share the same answer; a drawing of a geometric figure; a written description and the degree of the angles associated with the figure; fraction, percentage and decimal equivalents

English:
- Pairs: antonyms and synonyms
- Trios: three words that are the same part of speech (verbs, nouns, adjectives, prepositions, etc.), traits that describe the same character

Social Studies:
- Pairs: match leaders and countries, cities and states, famous people and cultures, events and dates
- Trios: three groups of cities located on the same continent, groups of famous people who lived in the same time period, objects and art associated with different countries, three map pieces that form a continent

Science:
- Pairs: names of chemical elements and their symbols
- Trios: three groups of animals and plants that belong to the same scientific genus or species

World Language:
- Pairs: images and matching vocabulary words
- Trios: three words associated with the same theme (clothing, school, sports, vacation, etc.); words that mean the same thing in different languages; holidays, historical events, famous people or traditions associated with the same country; the same verb conjugated in three different tenses

These grouping strategies have been adapted from *Conflict Resolution in the High School* by Carol Miller Lieber with Linda Lantieri and Tom Roderick (Educators for Social Responsibility, 1998).

Activators Index

World Languages

References

Bandura, A. (1986). *Social foundations of thought and action: A social cognitive theory.* Englewood Cliffs, NJ: Prentice Hall.

Becker, B. & Luthar, S. (2002). Social Emotional Factors Affecting Achievement Outcomes Among Disadvantaged Students: Closing the Achievement Gap. *Educational Psychologist, 37*(4) 197-214.

Benard, B. (2004). *Resiliency: What we have learned.* San Francisco: WestEd.

Bruner, J. S. (1960). *The process of education.* Cambridge, MA: Harvard University Press.

Cain, S. (2012). *Quiet: The power of introverts in a world that can't stop talking.* New York: Crown Publishing Group.

Caine, G., Caine, R. N., McClintic, C., & Klimek, K. (2005). *12 Brain/Mind learning principles in action: The fieldbook for making connections, teaching, and the human brain.* Thousand Oaks, CA: Corwin Press.

Catalano, R. F., & Hawkins, J. D. (1996). The social development model: A theory of antisocial behavior. In J. D. Hawkins (ed.), *Delinquency and crime: Current theories.* New York: Cambridge University Press.

Cavert, C., & Cavert, S. A. (2006). *Are you more like...?/What would it be like...?: A back-to-back book of anytime questions for anysize answers.* Bethany, OK: Wood 'N' Barnes Publishing.

Cervone, B., & Cushman, K. (2012). *Teachers at work: Six exemplars of everyday practice.* Retrieved from http://studentsatthecenter.org/sites/scl.dl-dev.com/files/Teachers%20at%20Work_0.pdf

Chen, Z. (1999). Schema induction in children's analogical problem solving. *Journal of Educational Psychology, 91*(4), 703-715.

Cognitive Coaching Seminars. Retrieved from http://www.cognitivecoaching.com/ccseminars.htm

Cohen, E. (1980). *A multi-ability approach to the integrated classroom.* Palo Alto, CA: Stanford University Center for Educational Research.

Cole, J.C., & McLeod, J.S. (1999). Children's writing ability: The impact of the pictorial stimulus. *Psychology in the Schools, 36*(4), 359-370.

Coleman, J. C., & Hendry, L. (1990). *The nature of adolescence.* London: Routledge.

Dagher, Z.R. (1995). Does the use of analogies contribute to conceptual change? *Science and Education, 78*(6), 601-614.

Dean, Ceri B., Hubbell, Elizabeth Ross, Pitler, Howard, Stone, B.J. (2012*). Classroom instruction that works* (2nd ed.). Alexandria, VA: ASCD.

Durlak, J. A., Weissberg, R. P., Dymnicki, A. B., Taylor, R. D. and Schellinger, K. B. (2011). The impact of enhancing students' social and emotional learning: A meta-analysis of school-based universal interventions. *Child Development, 82*, 405–432.

Goldenberg, C. (Summer 2008). Teaching English language learners: What the research does—and does not—say. *American Educator, 2* (2), 8-23, 42-44.

Goldstein, A. P. (1981). *Psychological skill training.* New York: Pergamon Press.

Goldstein, A. P. (1988). *The prepare curriculum: Teaching prosocial behavior.* Champaign, IL: Research Press.

Gottfried, G.M. (1998). Using metaphors as modifiers: Children's production of metaphoric compounds. *Journal of Child Language, 24*(3), 567-601.

Hannaford, C. (1995). *Smart moves: Why learning is not all in your head.* Alexander, NC: Great Ocean Publishers.

Hattie, J., & Timperley, H. (2007). The power of feedback. *Review of Educational Research, 77* (1), 5-13.

Henderson, N. (2002). *Resiliency in schools: Making it happen for students and educators.* Thousand Oaks, CA: Sage Publications.

Hill, J. & Flynn, K. (2006). *Classroom instruction that works with English language learners.* Alexandria, VA: ASCD.

Himmele, P. & Himmele. W. (2009). *The language-rich classroom: A research-based framework for teaching English language learners*. Alexandria, VA: ASCD.

Immordina-Yang, M. H., Christodoulou, J. A., & Singh, V. (2012). Rest is not idleness: Implications of the brain's default mode for human development and education. *Perspectives on Psychological Science, 7*(4), 352–364.

Immordino-Yang, M. H., & Faeth, M. (2010). The role of emotion and skilled intuition in learning. In D. A. Sousa (Ed.), *Mind, brain and education: Neuroscience implications for the classroom*. Bloomington, IN: Solution Tree Press.

Jensen, E. (1998). *Teaching with the brain in mind*. Alexandria, VA: ASCD.

Jensen, E. (2009). *Super teaching: Over 1000 practical strategies* (4th ed.). Thousand Oaks, CA: Corwin Press.

Johnson, D. W., & Johnson, R. T. (2000). Cooperative Learning: Two heads learn better than one, *In Context* 18, 1.

Jones, F., adapted by Marshall, K. (2010). Marshall Memo 331. April 12, 2010.

Jordan, L. Cognitive strategies. Retrieved from http://www.specialconnections.ku.edu/~kucrl/cgi-bin/drupal/?q=instruction/cognitive_strategies

Karpov, Y. V. (2003). Development through lifespan: A neo-Vygotskian approach. In A. Kozulin, B. Gindis, V. S. Ageyev, & S. M. Miller (Eds.), *Vygotsky's educational theory in cultural context*. New York: Cambridge University Press.

Klem, A. & Connell, J. (2004). Relationships matter: Linking teacher support to student engagement and achievement. *Journal of School Health, 74*(7), 262-273.

Kohn, A. (2004). Feel-bad education. *Education Week, 24*(3), 44–45.

Lemov, D. (2010). *Teach like a champion: 49 techniques that put students on the path to college,* Hoboken, NJ: Wiley.

Lieber, C. M. (2009). *Making learning real: Reaching and engaging all learners in secondary classrooms.* Cambridge, MA: Educators for Social Responsibility.

Lieber, C. M. (2009). *Getting classroom management right: Guided discipline and personalized support in secondary schools.* Cambridge, MA: Educators for Social Responsibility.

Lyman, F. (1981). The responsive classroom discussion: The inclusion of all students. *Mainstreaming Digest.* College Park, MD: University of Maryland College of Education.

Mason, L. (1994). Cognitive and metacognitive aspects in conceptual change by analogy. *Instructional Science, 22*(3), 157-187.

Mason, L. (1995). Analogy, meta-conceptual awareness and conceptual change: A classroom study. *Educational Studies, 20*(2), 267-291.

McTighe, J. & Wiggins, G. (2013). *Essential Questions.* Alexandria, VA: ASCD.

Medina, J. J. (2008). *Brain rules: 12 principles for surviving and thriving at work, home, and school.* Seattle, WA: Pear Press.

Phinney, J., & Ong, A. (2007). Conceptualization and measurement of ethnic identity: Current status and future directions. *Journal of Counseling Psychology, 54*(3).

Plummer, J. (2009). Elementary students' development of astronomy concepts in the planetarium. *Journal of Research in Science Teaching, 46*(2), 192–209.

Osher, D., Sprague, J., Weissberg, R. P., Axelrod, J., Keenan, S., Kendziora, K., & Zins, J. E. (2008). A comprehensive approach to promoting social, emotional, and academic growth in contemporary schools. *Best Practices in School Psychology, 4,* 1263-1278.

Ritchhart, R., Church, M., & Morrison, K. (2011). *Making thinking visible: How to promote engagement, understanding, and independence for all learners.* San Francisco: Jossey-Bass.

Rowe, M. B. (1987) Wait time: Slowing down may be a way of speeding up. *American Educator, 11*(1), 38-43,47.

Scruggs, T. E., Mastropieri M. A., Berkeley, S., & Graetz, J. (2010). Do special education interventions improve learning of secondary content? A meta-analysis. *Remedial and Special Education, 36*, 437-449.

Shute, V. J. (2008). Focus on formative feedback. *Review of Educational Research, 78*(1), 153-189.

Skloot, R. (April 2000). Henrietta's Dance. *Johns Hopkins Magazine*. Retrieved from http://www.jhu.edu/jhumag/0400web/01.html

Slavkin, M. (2004). *Authentic learning: How learning about the brain can shape the development of students.* Lanham, MD: Scarecrow Education.

Sousa, D. A., & Tomlinson, C. A. (2010). *Differentiation and the brain: How neuroscience supports the learner-friendly classroom.* Bloomington, IN: Solution Tree.

Sparks, S. D. (2012, September 26). Studies probe power of 'personalization.' *Education Week, 32*(5), 14-15.

Stevens, J.D. & Goldberg, D. (2001). *For the learners' sake: Brain-based instruction for the 21st century.* Brookline, MA: Zephyr Press.

Stahl, R.J. (1990). *Using "think time" behaviors to promote students' information processing, learning and on-task participation: An instructional manual.* Tempe, AZ: Arizona State University.

Tobin, K. (1987) The role of wait time in higher cognitive level learning. *Review of Educational Research, 57* (1), 69-95.

Tokuhama-Espinosa, T. (2008). *Living languages: Multilingualism across the lifespan.* Westport, CT: Greenwood.

Toshalis, E. & Nakkula, M.J. (2012). *Motivation, engagement, and student voice.* Retrieved from http://studentsatthecenter.org/sites/scl.dl-dev.com/files/Motivation%20Engagement%20Student%20Voice_0.pdf

University College London (2006). Novelty aids learning. *Science Daily*. Retrieved from http://www.sciencedaily.com/releases/2006/08/060804084518.htm

Vygotsky, L. S. (1978). *Mind in society: The development of higher psychological processes.* Cambridge, MA: Harvard University Press.

Walkington, C. (2013). Using adaptive learning technologies to personalize instruction to student interests: The impact of relevant contexts on performance and learning outcomes. *Journal of Educational Psychology*, Special Issue on Advanced Learning Technologies.

Walsh, J. A. & Sattes, B.D. (2011). *Thinking through quality questioning: Deepening student engagement.* Thousand Oaks, CA: Corwin Press.

Willis, J.A., (Summer 2007). The Neuroscience of joyful learning. *Educational Leadership, 64*. Retrieved from http://www.ascd.org/publications/educational-leadership/summer07/vol64/num09/The-Neuroscience-of-Joyful-Education.aspx

Zadina, J. (Spring 2009). The multiple pathways model: Addressing multiple pathways in the brain to enhance language learning. *Idiom, 39,* (1). Retrieved from http://idiom.nystesol.org/articles/vol39-01.html

Zimmerman, B.J. (2001). Theories of Self-Regulated Learning and Academic Achievement: An Overview and Analysis. In Zimmerman, B.J. & Schunk, D.H. (Eds.), *Self-regulated learning and academic achievement: Theoretical perspectives.* Mahwah, NJ: Lawrence Erlbaum Associates.

Credits

Chapter 4 – Foundational Activators

Turn and Talk geometry example from *CPM Educational Program, Mathematics 2 (Geometry)*, second edition, copyright 2001, used with permission.

Turn and Talk Article biology example cites *Scientific American* "Sea Otters Fight Global Warming" podcast by Sophie Bushwick, podcast transcript online at http://www.scientificamerican.com/podcast/episode.cfm?id=sea-otters-fight-global-warming-12-09-14

Turn and Talk chemistry question adapted from Quizfarm, http://quizfarm.com/quizzes/Element/matseb2611/which-chemical-element-is-your-personality-most-like-10-elements/

Turn and Talk ELA Reading – Literature question adapted from "English 11 Summer Reading Assessment: *The Namesake*," Cambridge Public Schools, http://www3.cpsd.us/media/theme/Pro-Cambridge/network/10516/media/CPS%20Redesign/documents/English/English_11_Socratic_Seminar_Questions.pdf?rev=0

Popcorn/Wave ELA Reading – Literature question adapted from Somebody/Wanted/But/So framework in *Responses to Literature* by J. MacOn, D. Bewell, and M. Vogt, International Reading Association, 1991.

Turn and Talk ELA Language question adapted from National Council of Teachers of English website, http://www.ncte.org/positions/statements/genderfairuseoflang

Chapter 6 – Post It Up

Earth Science career option list adapted from "Earth Science Careers," National Aeronautics and Space Administration website, http://climate2.jpl.nasa.gov/eswSite/eswCareers/

ELA Reading – Literature example adapted from *The Language-Rich Classroom: A Research-Based Framework for Teaching English Language Learners* by P. Himmele and W. Himmele, ASCD, 2009.

Chapter 7 – Silent Conversation

Geometry example from *CPM Educational Program, Mathematics 2 (Geometry)*, second edition, copyright 2001, used with permission.

Biology example cites "Henrietta's Dance," article by Rebecca Skloot in *Johns Hopkins Magazine,* April 2000, found at http://www.jhu.edu/~jhumag/0400web/01.html

ELA Reading: Literature question adapted from Wikia Webinar website, http://holden.wikia.com/wiki/What's_bothering_Holden

Chapter 8 – Mini Whiteboard

ELA Writing example cites Google Search Education, http://www.google.com/insidesearch/searcheducation/

ELA Reading – Informational Texts prompt adapted from *Pathways to the Common Core* by L. Calkins, M. Ehrenworth, and C. Lehman, Heinemann, 2012.

ELA Speaking and Listening prompt adapted from Common Sense Media, http://www.commonsensemedia.org/educators/blog/does-the-internet-amplify-gender-stereotypes

Chapter 9 – Card Sorts

Geometry examples (available at http://www.esrnational.org/activators) created by Winston Gayle, Queens Preparatory Academy, Queens, New York, used with permission.

Biology example adapted from Humboldt County Office of Education website, http://scorescience.humboldt.k12.ca.us/fast/teachers/Internauts/teacherpage.htm

Physics example adapted from Ohio Department of Education, http://ims.ode.state.oh.us/ODE/IMS/Lessons/Content/CSC_LP_S03_BG_L09_I19_01.pdf

ELA Reading – Informational Texts prompt adapted from KCK Literacy Curriculum website, https://kckliteracycurriculum.wikispaces.com/file/detail/6th+Grade+Activities+and+questions+to+drive+Clusters+of+standards.docx

Chapter 10 – Toss One, Take One

Physics example adapted from *Conceptual Physics* by P.G. Hewitt, Pearson Education, 2002

ELA Reading – Literature example adapted from Virginia Commonwealth University American Romanticism class blog, http://wp.vcu.edu/engl37212a/2012/03/18/class-blog-for-the-narrative-of-the-life-of-frederick-douglass/

Chapter 12 – Opinion Continuum

Algebra example adapted from Math Planet, http://www.mathplanet.com/education/algebra-1/systems-of-linear-equations-and-inequalities/the-substitution-method-for-solving-linear-systems

Geometry example from *CPM Educational Program, Mathematics 2 (Geometry)*, second edition, copyright 2001, used with permission.

Biology prompt adapted from Bright Hub Education website, http://www.brighthubeducation.com/middle-school-social-studies-lessons/109157-pros-and-cons-of-genetically-modified-foods-debate-lesson/

Chapter 13 – Four (or more) Corners

Geometry example from *Glencoe McGraw-Hill Quick Review Math Handbook*, McGraw-Hill, 2010, used with permission.

Biology prompt adapted from Eau Claire Area School District website, http://www.ecasd.k12.wi.us/faculty/mallen/DiseasesAssignment.pdf

Physics example adapted from Physics Classroom, http://www.physicsclassroom.com/class/newtlaws/u2l1a.cfm

ELA Reading – Literature prompt adapted from Wikispaces website, http://inthetimeofthebutterflies2011.wikispaces.com/Theme

Chapter 15 – Moving Line-Up

Geometry example from *CPM Educational Program, Mathematics 2 (Geometry)*, second edition, copyright 2001, used with permission.

Physics questions adapted from *Conceptual Physics* by P.G. Hewitt, Pearson Education, 2002.

ELA Reading – Literature questions adapted from National Endowment for the Arts: The Big Read website, http://www.neabigread.org/books/fahrenheit451/fahrenheit451_03.php

ELA Reading – Informational Texts article citation from *New York Times*, "On Road to Recovery, Past Adversity Provides a Map," http://www.nytimes.com/2011/01/04/health/04mind.html

Chapter 16 – Rotation Stations

Algebra example adapted from I Love Math, http://www.ilovemath.org/index.php?option=com_docman&task=doc_download&gid=121&Itemid=31

Geometry example adapted from Teaching Channel, https//www.teachingchannel.org/videos/carousel-activity-math-lesson

Biology example adapted from Readingquest.org, http://www.readingquest.org/strat/carousel.html

Chemistry example adapted from Cherry Hill High School East Chemistry web archive: http://east.chclc.org/eastsci/

Physics example adapted from Colina Middle Schools website, http://colinamiddle.net/dmatras/Chapter%2010/pages/Friction%20Lab.pdf

ELA Writing example adapted from StudyMode, http://www.studymode.com/essays/

ELA Reading – Informational Texts example adapted from New York Times Learning Network, http://learning.blogs.nytimes.com

ELA Speaking and Listening example adapted from Logical Fallacies Quizlet, http://quizlet.com/2140673/print/

Chapter 17 – Mix and Mingle

Geometry example from *CPM Educational Program, Mathematics 2 (Geometry)*, second edition, copyright 2001, used with permission.

Physics example adapted from *Conceptual Physics* by P.G. Hewitt, Pearson Education, 2002.

ELA Speaking and Listening example adapted from Learning to Give, http://learningtogive.org/lessons/unit232/lesson4.html

ELA Language example adapted from BetterLesson, "Greek Root Words I" PowerPoint presentation, http://betterlesson.com/document/1376000/greek-root-words-i-pptx

About the Authors

Nicole Frazier joined ESR as a program consultant and author in 2009. Nicole supports middle and high schools across the country in the areas of instruction, data-driven decision making, professional development, advisory, postsecondary supports, and freshman orientation and intervention programs. Her experience is wide-ranging; in addition to serving as a high school educator for 13 years in diverse high schools in large and small cities, Nicole has worked with urban at-risk youth, rural schools, English language learners, high-performing large comprehensive high schools, and small turnaround schools. With ESR, Nicole helps leadership teams and faculty develop schoolwide systems and practices that support teaching and learning to build an intentional academic culture. Nicole is the producer, director, and co-author of *Getting Advisory Right: Tools for Supporting Effective Advisories,* a four-disc DVD set released by ESR in 2011. Nicole lives with her family in Denver, Colorado.

After over 15 years teaching, mostly in New York City public high schools, **Donna Mehle** joined ESR in 2008 as a program consultant and author. In addition to her work in the classroom, Donna served as a literacy coach, advisory program coordinator, school leadership team member, New York City Writing Project seminar coordinator and English Department facilitator. As an ESR consultant, Donna supports districts, schools and teachers around the country with student-centered teaching and learning, advisory program design and development, and classroom management and discipline. Donna lives with her husband in Morrisville, Pennsylvania.

About Educators for Social Responsibility

Founded in 1982, ESR is a national leader in school reform. ESR provides professional development, consultation, and educational resources to adults who teach young people in preschool through high school.

ESR creates, disseminates, and teaches core practices that:

1. Reduce educational disparities and facilitate equal access to quality instruction and opportunities for students. ESR helps schools build a positive climate and culture; a disciplined and supportive learning environment; and personalized, high-achieving classrooms that promote healthy development and academic success for all students.

2. Help students develop and strengthen social skills, emotional competencies, and qualities of character that increase personal and interpersonal efficacy and cultivate social responsibility. ESR helps schools build high quality social and emotional learning programs and initiatives that promote respect and help to reduce intolerance, harassment and bullying, and risky and aggressive student behaviors.

ESR has a long history and a wealth of experience facilitating the change process and much practical expertise in how to create positive learning environments in today's schools. Our work with principals, school leadership teams, faculty members, students, and families is informed by current research and the best practices in educational leadership, instruction, discipline and student support and youth development.

Visit us online at http://www.esrnational.org for more information about additional ESR products and services and to sign up for our monthly e-newsletter.

We can be reached at:

esr

Educators for Social Responsibility
23 Garden Street
Cambridge, MA 02138
617-492-1764 (phone)
617-864-5164 (fax)
educators@esrnational.org